ECONOMIC DEVELOPMENT IN

AFRICA

REPORT 2016

DEBT DYNAMICS AND DEVELOPMENT FINANCE IN AFRICA

UNITED NATIONS
New York and Geneva, 2016

NOTE

Symbols of United Nations documents are composed of capital letters combined with figures. Mention of such a symbol indicates a reference to a United Nations document.

The designations employed and the presentation of the material do not imply the expression of any opinion on the part of the United Nations concerning the legal status of any country, territory, city or area, or of authorities or concerning the delimitation of its frontiers or boundaries.

Material in this publication may be freely quoted or reprinted, but acknowledgement is requested, together with a copy of the publication containing the quotation or reprint to be sent to the UNCTAD secretariat.

UNCTAD/ALDC/AFRICA/2016

UNITED NATIONS PUBLICATION
Sales No. E.16.II.D.3
ISBN 978-92-1-112900-7
eISBN 978-92-1-058056-4
ISSN 1990–5114

ACKNOWLEDGEMENTS

The *Economic Development in Africa Report 2016: Debt Dynamics and Development Finance in Africa*, was prepared by a team of UNCTAD contributors, headed by Junior Roy Davis, and composed of the following people: Bineswaree Bolaky, Ange Bella Ndayisenga, Laura Páez and Claudia Roethlisberger. The work was completed under the overall supervision of Taffere Tesfachew, Director of the Division for Africa, Least Developed Countries and Special Programmes of UNCTAD.

An ad hoc expert group meeting on debt dynamics and development finance in Africa was held in Geneva on 19 and 20 January 2016 to conduct a peer review of the report. The meeting brought together specialists in African debt and development finance. Those participating in the meeting were Raphael Otieno, Director, Macroeconomic and Financial Management Institute of Eastern and Southern Africa; Annalisa Prizzon, Research Fellow, Overseas Development Institute; and Bernhard Gunter, Professor, American University, Washington, D.C. Also present were members of the *Economic Development in Africa Report* team. The following UNCTAD staff members took part and/or made comments on the draft: Stephanie Blankenburg, Lisa Borgatti, Mussie Delelegn, Kristine Fitzpatrick, Samuel Gayi, Ricardo Gottschalk, Christian Kingombe, Joerg Mayer, Jean-Claude Mporamazina, Janvier Nkurunziza, Hafiz Mirza, Patrick Nwokedi Osakwe, Amelia Santos-Paulino, Rolf Traeger and Anida Yupari.

Statistical assistance was provided by Agnès Collardeau-Angleys. Stefanie West provided secretarial support. Nadège Hadjemian designed the cover. Deniz Barki and Lucy Délèze-Black edited the report.

Madasamyraja Rajalingam did the layout, graphics and desktop publishing.

CONTENTS

BOXES

FIGURES

TABLES

EXPLANATORY NOTES

The $ sign refers to the United States dollar.

Sub-Saharan Africa: Except where otherwise stated, this includes South Africa.

North Africa: In this publication, the Sudan is classified as part of sub-Saharan Africa, not North Africa.

Two dots (..) indicate that the data are either not available or not applicable.

ABBREVIATIONS

ASYCUDA	Automated System for Customs Data
BRICS	Brazil, China, India, the Russian Federation and South Africa
COMESA	Common Market for Eastern and Southern Africa
FDI	foreign direct investment
GDP	gross domestic product
GNI	gross national income
HIPC	heavily indebted poor country
IMF	International Monetary Fund
LDC	least developed country
LIC	low-income country
LMC	lower middle-income country
MDRI	Multilateral Debt Relief Initiative
ODA	official development assistance
OECD	Organization for Economic Cooperation and Development
PPP	public–private partnership
UNCTAD	United Nations Conference on Trade and Development

INTRODUCTION

Africa has major development aspirations in the broader context of a global and continental economic development agenda. This calls for substantial financial resources at a time when the global development finance landscape is changing, from a model centred on official development assistance and the coverage of remaining financing needs through external debt, to a framework with greater emphasis on the mobilization of domestic resources. The Economic Development in Africa Report 2016 examines some of the key policy issues that underlie Africa's domestic and external debt, and provides policy guidance on the delicate balance required between financing development alternatives and overall debt sustainability. This report analyses Africa's international debt exposure and how domestic debt is increasingly playing a role in some African countries as a development finance option, and also examines complementary financing options and how they relate to debt.

Following debt relief under the Heavily Indebted Poor Countries Initiative and Multilateral Debt Relief Initiative over the past two decades, external debt in several African countries has rapidly increased in recent years and is becoming a source of concern to policymakers, analysts and multilateral financial institutions. While Africa's current external debt ratios currently appear manageable, their rapid growth in several countries is a concern and requires action if a recurrence of the African debt crisis of the late 1980s and the 1990s is to be avoided. In 2011–2013, the annual average external debt stock of Africa amounted to $443 billion (22.0 per cent of gross national income (GNI)). Africa's external debt stock grew rapidly, by on average 10.2 per cent per year in 2011–2013, compared with 7.8 per cent per year in 2006–2009. The burgeoning debt of several African countries may be explained by the fact that they currently have better access to international financial markets, as Africa has registered robust levels of economic growth over the past decade. In this regard, investors are seeking better yields and higher rates of return[1] based on the perceived risk of investing in Africa (given low-yield asset investment in advanced countries). The rise of other developing countries, particularly the group of Brazil, China, India, the Russian Federation and South Africa, commonly known as the BRICS countries, has also opened up new sources of external finance that African countries may take advantage of, often without the imposition of conditionalities. As a result of this favourable external environment, some African countries have successfully issued sovereign bonds since the mid-2000s. However, the favourable environment that contributed to the decline in debt ratios has changed. For instance, risks associated with commodity exporters have risen, and their borrowing costs have increased sharply.

The size and rate of growth of Africa's external debt also have implications for sustainability. Some Governments are currently borrowing from private lenders, in contrast to previous years when they borrowed mostly from official lenders with concessional terms. Some African countries have borrowed syndicated loans while others have issued Eurobonds. In addition, the private sector in Africa is also accumulating external debt. For example, large corporate bonds have been issued in Nigeria and South Africa. As these bonds are in foreign currencies, countries become susceptible to foreign exchange risks. In addition, private sector debt may translate into public debt if bailouts become necessary to prevent a collapse of the financial system when private borrowers cannot honour their debt obligations. Furthermore, (non-concessional) borrowing from private lenders is challenging because renegotiation is generally more difficult when a country is unable to service its debt, and conditions for renegotiation come at a very high cost. Although these dynamics are not exclusive to private lenders, borrowing from private lenders also exposes African countries to litigation by vulture funds and investment arbitration. It is therefore necessary for African Governments to closely monitor evolving debt characteristics and take pre-emptive actions to avoid potential debt distress.

Domestic debt and debt markets have also witnessed significant developments. Until recently, the literature on sovereign borrowing and debt dynamics had largely overlooked the role domestic debt could play in financing development in Africa and focused almost exclusively on external debt. In recent years, however, several countries in the region have looked increasingly to domestic sources when expanding their net borrowing and adopted policies aimed at developing domestic debt markets with the active support of international financial institutions and other international organizations. In the future, domestic borrowing is likely to play an increasingly significant role as sustained growth performance in a large group of African countries boosts national savings and broadens the scope for financing development with domestic resources. It will also be important for countries to find ways of productively utilizing additional liquidity in domestic financial institutions, which did not always occur in the past.

With domestic debt playing an increasingly important role, countries will face new risks as the numbers of creditors and debt instruments continue to expand. Owing to its size and swift growth, the consideration of domestic debt will become important in assessing public debt sustainability. Other concerns with regard to domestic debt accumulation include the following: the expansion of public sector borrowing in domestic markets may crowd out private sector investments, given the shallow financial markets and low levels of domestic savings common in the region (although institutional savings have been higher); and borrowing in the domestic market is often perceived as being inconsistent with prospects of achieving and preserving public debt sustainability. Financial liberalization and related reforms adopted since the mid-1980s have resulted in increased domestic real interest rates. As a result, there are concerns that domestic borrowing may induce elements of macroeconomic instability in African economies and that the high interest burden may absorb a significant portion of government revenues, crowding out pro-poor and growth-enhancing spending (Abbas and Christensen, 2007). This has significant implications for women and children, who often bear the brunt of major reductions in social expenditure.

Given that in the 1990s, most African countries had relatively easy access to external financing in the form of concessional loans and grants, Governments have tended to avoid seemingly expensive domestic borrowing. Despite a long history of high fiscal deficits and a growing need for developmental and structural investments, Africa's bond markets have largely remained underdeveloped, mainly due to credibility issues. It is only in recent years that some countries have made substantial efforts to develop their domestic debt markets as they become increasingly reliant on them not only for development finance but also for financing fiscal deficits. This has acquired increased importance for five reasons.

First, in 2015, the adoption of two important United Nations resolutions, endorsed by world leaders, marked a milestone in terms of setting the international agenda for development in the years to come. The 2030 Agenda for Sustainable Development sets the Sustainable Development Goals that countries aspire to achieve in the next 15 years, and the Addis Ababa Action Agenda (A/RES/69/313), an outcome of the Third International Conference on Financing for Development, held in Addis Ababa in July 2015, sets the agenda and means of implementation for development finance. Both resolutions contain interrelated goals and commitments on sustainable financing for development, which have a bearing on Africa's development. These resolutions reflect a shift in emphasis from global development finance based on a model predominantly centred on official development assistance to a new global framework that places greater importance on domestic sources of finance, while maintaining public finance as a fundamental basis for achieving the Sustainable Development Goals. This poses an important financing challenge for African Governments; it is estimated by various sources that the required investment to finance the Goals in Africa could amount to between

$600 billion and $1.2 trillion per year (Chinzana et al., 2015; Schmidt-Traub, 2015; United Nations Conference on Trade and Development (UNCTAD), 2014). Africa's public budgetary resources are inadequate to address this need, and development partners will need to share the burden.

Second, it may no longer be presumed that external assistance, whether concessional debt or grants, will continue to play a key role in financing poverty reduction, the Sustainable Development Goals and growth-enhancing programmes in the foreseeable future. With recurring global financial crises and increased fiscal austerity, concerns have emerged that traditional donor funds may become more scarce and, therefore, having sufficiently liquid domestic bond markets is becoming increasingly unavoidable. Development challenges have also evolved, with the donor community paying increasing attention (and thus devoting increasing resources) to issues such as climate change and disaster prevention, which did not feature prominently in the development agenda a decade ago (United Nations Economic Commission for Africa, 2015).

Third, some African countries have recently transitioned to middle-income status (World Bank, 2016a). Concessional financing from the soft windows of multilateral development banks is therefore likely to be phased out in the future, as development partners divert more budgetary resources towards the poorer and more vulnerable countries. In other words, a transition to middle-income status means that financing becomes more expensive for such Governments, which have to rely more extensively on non-concessional or less concessional public and private financing sources.

Fourth, as many African countries are commodity dependent, external debt sustainability is also subject to the boom and bust cycles of international commodity markets and the associated fiscal squeeze countries experience when expected revenues fall. The current collapse in commodity prices provides evidence of this. The apparent end of the upward phase of the commodity price super cycle has translated into lower revenues from Africa's commodity exports. In short, Africa needs to be less dependent on volatile commodity markets.

Fifth, the global economic outlook remains gloomy, as fiscal austerity underpins the deceleration in growth in the eurozone, and China is shifting to a growth strategy that implies lower but more sustainable growth rates and a rebalancing of economic activity away from investment and manufacturing towards consumption and services. Manufacturing activity and trade also remain weak globally, reflecting not only developments in China, but also subdued global demand and investment more broadly, which could have a negative effect on Africa's development prospects. The recent instability in China's economy will most likely translate into lessened demand for African commodities, lower lending volumes and possibly higher interest rates.

Against this backdrop, Africa must critically assess its capacity to tackle its significant development challenges in light of its development finance requirements. This entails a redoubling of efforts to harness potential and innovative sources of finance, including those that may come from the private sector, such as through public–private partnerships, while also tackling rising levels of debt. Africa and its partners will also need to revisit existing debt sustainability frameworks. Debt sustainability is critical for Africa as it seeks to implement the Addis Ababa Action Agenda, achieve the Sustainable Development Goals and sustainably transform the continent.

A. MAIN FOCUS AND FINDINGS OF THIS REPORT

Some of the key questions addressed in this report are as follows:

- Following the Third International Conference on Financing for Development and the United Nations summit for the adoption of the post-2015 development agenda, how should African countries balance the multiple objectives of financing development spending and avoiding a debt crisis?

- What are the main external debt trends and the key drivers of these trends? How can the global financial architecture support countries in managing their debts sustainably?

- What are the current trends in public domestic debt in Africa? What are the main risk factors and opportunities at present, and how can the risks best be managed?

- What complementary modalities of finance are available to help Africa sustainably address critical development finance needs?

The five main findings presented in this report are summarized below.

First, given the complexity of Africa's development challenges, the scale of its development finance needs and the size of its capacity constraints, African countries need to leverage all possible sources of finance. Debt, both domestic and external, as well as other complementary sources, cannot be excluded from Africa's list of development finance policy options. Therefore, debt channelled to investments related to the Sustainable Development Goals should be afforded more flexibility. However, Africa's vulnerability to rapidly changing external conditions, including volatile commodity markets and unstable international financial markets, make debt a more problematic financing instrument than necessary.

Second, external debt in Africa is on the rise and is predominantly related to reduced export revenue, a widening current account deficit and slower economic growth. The composition, terms and conditions of such debt are changing, with higher interest rates and concessional loans as a share of total debt. The structure and composition of debt are therefore relevant to debt sustainability.

Third, domestic debt in Africa is gradually rising and increasingly consists of marketable debt. Domestic capital markets have been deepening as international investor interest has grown. Greater reliance on domestic resources may allow countries more policy space in implementing their development priorities, as financing through official development assistance is often tied to policy conditionalities. However, with domestic debt playing an increasingly important role, countries may face new risks as the range of creditors and debt instruments continues to expand.

Fourth, there is a wide range of complementary modalities of development finance, which, if effectively tapped, may contribute to meeting Africa's financing needs without necessarily affecting debt sustainability. Such modalities include remittances and public–private partnerships, as well as curtailing illicit financial flows.

Fifth, enhanced international and regional cooperation is needed to build institutional capacity in addressing Africa's development finance needs and debt management challenges. Regional integration could play a critical role in coordinating and mainstreaming key regulatory and institutional dimensions of broader financing for development initiatives in the context of Agenda 2063 of the African Union and the 2030 Agenda for Sustainable Development.

B. ORGANIZATION OF THE REPORT

This report is comprised of four chapters and a conclusion. Chapter 1 considers the financing needs of African countries in light of their national and regional development plans and global commitments. It examines the changing development finance landscape in Africa including, notably, the Sustainable Development Goals, the Addis Ababa Action Agenda and Agenda 2063, and the implications of these aspirations for Africa's debt sustainability. Chapter 2 examines some key trends and patterns and the composition of external debt in Africa, and then discusses debt sustainability and revisits current debt sustainability frameworks in more detail. Chapter 3 considers the increasing importance of domestic debt in Africa by analysing its trends, patterns and compositions. It presents five detailed case studies of domestic debt in Ghana, Kenya, Nigeria, the United Republic of Tanzania and Zambia. Chapter 4 discusses complementary modalities of finance for Africa's development and focuses on three modalities that have a limited impact on or improve debt sustainability. It examines the role and potential of public–private partnerships for infrastructure financing, how remittances can contribute to development finance and how illicit financial flows may be curtailed. The conclusion in chapter 5 offers policy recommendations that focus on how African countries may avoid the risk of debt distress arising especially from domestic financing and other initiatives such as public–private partnerships. The policy recommendations also address the roles that African Governments, external partners and the international community can play in ensuring that Africa's public debt remains sustainable.

CHAPTER **1**

ADDRESSING AFRICA'S DEVELOPMENT FINANCE NEEDS

A. INTRODUCTION

This chapter first examines Africa's growing financing needs and changes in the development finance landscape of Africa. It then highlights the financing requirements of Africa in the context of the Sustainable Development Goals and Agenda 2063, and concludes with a discussion about the scope and limitations of official development assistance as a source of development finance.

B. SCOPE OF FINANCING REQUIREMENTS

Several important international developments occurred in 2015 that will have significant implications for the scale of Africa's financing needs and debt sustainability. In September 2015, the international community adopted the Sustainable Development Goals. African Member States have thereby committed to implementing national and regional development programmes in the next 15 years that aim to contribute to achieving the 17 Goals and 169 targets. Compared with the eight Millennium Development Goals and 21 targets, this international engagement is a far more ambitious development endeavour that will necessitate substantial financial resources. Most of the studies cited in this section highlight the difficulty of estimating financing needs in Africa related to the Sustainable Development Goals. The studies vary in methodologies and underlying scenario assumptions. Given the complexity, scope and differences in methodology, it is difficult to make a direct comparison between the estimates presented in (table 1).

A recent analysis of available sector studies by Schmidt-Traub (2015) shows that incremental spending needs for achieving the Sustainable Development Goals in low-income countries and lower middle-income countries[2] may amount to $1.2 trillion per year ($342 billion–$355 billion for low-income countries and $903 billion–$938 billion for lower middle-income countries). For 2015–2030, this corresponds to 11 per cent of gross domestic product (GDP), measured using market exchange rates. Schmidt-Traub (2015) does not provide estimates by region. However, using the estimates for all low-income countries to estimate the incremental costs for achieving the Sustainable Development Goals in African low-income countries gives a total of $269 billion–$279 billion per year (the share of GDP of African low-income countries in GDP of all low-income countries is 78.5 per cent). Similarly, using the estimates for all lower middle-income countries to estimate the incremental financing needs related to the Sustainable

Table 1. Estimates of financing requirements for Africa related to the Sustainable Development Goals		
Source	**Estimated amount per year**	**Scope of estimate**
International Energy Agency (2012)	$25 billion	Amount needed to achieve universal access to modern energy services by 2030
World Bank (2012)	$18 billion	Cost of climate change adaptation
UNCTAD (2014)	$210 billion	Amount needed for basic infrastructure, food security, health, education and climate change mitigation
Chinzana et al. (2015)	$1.2 trillion	Additional investment required to meet Goal 1
Schmidt-Traub (2015)	$614 billion–$638 billion	Incremental financing needs related to the Sustainable Development Goals
World Bank (2015a)	$93 billion	Amount needed for infrastructure

Development Goals in African lower middle-income countries gives a total of $345 billion–$359 billion per year. In total, therefore, the incremental costs of financing the Sustainable Development Goals in Africa may amount to $614 billion–$638 billion per year.

Chinzana et al. (2015) focus on Goal 1 (end poverty) and estimate the level of additional investment that Africa will require to meet the Goal, assuming that savings, official development assistance and foreign direct investment remain at current levels, given that Africa will require a GDP growth rate of 16.6 per cent per year in 2015–2030 to achieve Goal 1 by 2030. Based on Africa's nominal GDP in 2015, this corresponds to an investment–GDP ratio of 87.5 per cent per year ($1.7 trillion) and a financing gap–GDP ratio of 65.6 per cent per year ($1.2 trillion). However, the results vary widely across subregions and individual countries and based on levels of development.

Preliminary forecasts by UNCTAD show that total investment needs at a global level to achieve the Sustainable Development Goals could reach $5 trillion–$7 trillion per year during the 15-year delivery period (UNCTAD, 2014). Investment needs in key sectors of developing countries related to the Goals could reach $3.3 trillion–$4.5 trillion per year for basic infrastructure (roads, rail and ports; power stations; and water and sanitation), food security (agriculture and rural development), climate change mitigation and adaptation, health and education. At current investment levels (both public and private) of $1.4 trillion per year in Sustainable Development Goals-related sectors, an annual funding gap of up to $2.5 trillion would remain in developing countries. Based on Africa's current share of nominal GDP in GDP of developing countries (around 8.4 per cent, based on UNCTADStat figures for 2013), this implies an annual funding gap of up to $210 billion in African countries. This is likely a conservative estimate for African countries; given that their share of GDP is low and that their infrastructure deficit is higher than that of most of the other developing countries, their share of resources should be much higher.

The World Bank (2012) estimates that investment needs in infrastructure alone amount to $93 billion per year in Africa. Average private sector participation in current infrastructure investment in developing countries is considerably lower than that in developed countries and may not address existing investment needs without significant upscaling (African Union et al., 2010).

In 2015, the African Development Bank initiated the infrastructure fund Africa50, which aims to increase the level of investment funds channelled into national and regional projects in the energy, transport, information and communications technology and water sectors. For example, the Fund intends to mobilize over $100 billion for infrastructure development, from the stock market, African central bank reserves and African diaspora, and will target lending to the private sector to enhance their participation in the development of the economy. This will help develop Africa's infrastructure by lending to high-return infrastructure development investments to unlock its economic potential.

Data from the Programme for Infrastructure Development in Africa and Africa Infrastructure Country Diagnostic study show that African countries lag behind other developing regions in terms of measures of infrastructure coverage, such as road, rail and telephone density, power generation capacity and service coverage. While lower middle-income countries and resource-rich countries could meet their infrastructure needs with an attainable commitment of 10–12 per cent of GDP, low-income countries need to devote 25–36 per cent of GDP (World Bank, 2015b).

While infrastructure investment needs are already large, including requirements related to the other Sustainable Development Goals raises this number higher. Estimates made prior to the United Nations Conference on Sustainable Development, held in Rio de Janeiro, Brazil in June 2012, determined that Africa would require close to $200 billion per year to implement sustainable development commitments under the social, economic and environmental dimensions (United Nations Economic Commission for Africa, 2015).

C. ROLE OF RESOURCE MOBILIZATION
IN THE CONTEXT OF DEVELOPMENT FINANCE

African leaders committed in 2013 to implementing the continental development vision in Agenda 2063 (box 1), followed in January 2015 by the adoption of a first 10-year plan of action for Agenda 2063. Agenda 2063 sets out seven aspirations for Africa and emphasizes that it needs to become self-reliant and finance its own development while building accountable institutions and States at all levels (African Union, 2015). An important objective is for African countries to finance their development through the mobilization of domestic resources (savings and taxes), accompanied by a deepened and enhanced use of capital markets (both equity and debt), while maintaining debt levels within sustainable limits.

Box 1. Agenda 2063: The Africa We Want

Agenda 2063 delineates the vision of African leaders of "an integrated, prosperous and peaceful Africa, driven by its own citizens and representing a dynamic force in the international arena" (African Union, 2015). It serves as a road map for Africa's development until 2063 that is committed to achieving the following seven aspirations:

- A prosperous Africa based on inclusive growth and sustainable development
- An integrated continent, politically united based on the ideals of pan-Africanism and the vision of Africa's renaissance
- An Africa of good governance, democracy, respect for human rights, justice and the rule of law
- A peaceful and secure Africa
- An Africa with a strong cultural identity, common heritage, values and ethics
- An Africa whose development is people-driven, relying on the potential of African people, especially its women and youth, and caring for children
- Africa as a strong, united, resilient and influential global player and partner

Agenda 2063 calls for strengthening domestic resource mobilization, building continental capital markets and financial institutions and reversing illicit flows of capital from the continent, with a view to achieving the following by 2025:

- Reducing aid dependency by 50 per cent
- Eliminating all forms of illicit flows
- Doubling the contribution of African capital markets in development finance
- Rendering fully operational the African Remittances Institute
- Reducing unsustainable levels of debt, heavy indebtedness and odious debt
- Building effective, transparent and harmonized tax and revenue collection systems and public expenditure

The Addis Ababa Action Agenda places a large part of the financial burden for achieving the Sustainable Development Goals in developing countries on their own financial resources, stating that "for all countries, public policies and the mobilization and effective use of domestic resources, underscored by the principle of national ownership, are central to our common pursuit of sustainable development", including achieving the Goals (para. 20).[3] The Agenda also highlights the need for developing countries to develop domestic capital markets, particularly long-term bond and insurance markets to meet longer term financing needs (para. 44) and recognizes the importance of borrowing as a tool for developing countries to finance investment critical to achieving sustainable development, including the Goals, but states that such borrowing must be managed prudently and that many countries remain vulnerable to debt crises (para. 93). Finally, the Agenda states that "maintaining sustainable debt levels is the responsibility of the borrowing countries", while "lenders also have a responsibility to lend in a way that does not undermine a country's debt sustainability" (para. 97). Africa stands at a crossroads in this respect, as it will need to borrow from both domestic and external sources at a time when external shocks are eroding its debt carrying and servicing capacity. The recent slump in commodity prices has negatively impacted commodity exporting countries and this may undermine their debt sustainability.

Both Agenda 2063 and the Addis Ababa Action Agenda recognize the importance of augmenting capacities for domestic resource mobilization to finance Africa's development. Domestic resources mainly include tax revenues and private savings (both household and corporate). However, such mobilization is not only about mobilizing domestic resources, but should also encompass incentives to retain domestic savings within domestic borders and allocate such funds effectively to productive uses. While tax revenues have recently increased, from $123.1 billion in 2002 to $508.3 billion in 2013, most of this increase was driven by resource-rich countries that rely on resource rents. Private savings rates, in contrast, have remained relatively low in Africa, especially sub-Saharan Africa, compared with East Asia and the Pacific (African Capacity-Building Foundation, 2015). Furthermore, a critical concern with regard to domestic resource mobilization is how to retain domestic savings within domestic borders for financing domestic investment, rather than letting such savings leak out of African national and regional borders. This is clearly related to curtailing illicit financial flows.[4] In this context, the development of financial markets in Africa should be fostered and accompanied by an augmentation of domestic investment opportunities, in line with the 2030 Agenda for Sustainable Development. For example, in some lower middle-income countries in Africa, the creation of stock markets both nationally and regionally can mobilize domestic savings to finance the expansion of investment and trade operations by public and private commercial enterprises.[5] The same functions may also be performed by the issuance of government-guaranteed domestic and regional bonds to finance infrastructure and trade development. For domestic resources such as savings to remain within African borders, African savings agents need domestic instruments to which they can channel their savings and need to bring the risk–return profiles of domestic instruments close to those of regional and international financial markets. Such instruments may include deposits at Africa-based financial institutions such as commercial banks and development banks, pension funds and equity shares, as well as high-yield domestic debt instruments.

In 2008, the African Development Bank launched an African financial markets initiative to stimulate the use of local currency bond markets in Africa. Through its African domestic bonds fund, the Bank seeks to support the creation of sound domestic debt markets in Africa. Similarly, the Eastern and Southern African Trade and Development Bank, a treaty-based regional institution established in 1985, has among its objectives to foster the development and deepening of financial and capital markets in member States. The planning and coordinating agency of the New Partnership for Africa's Development highlights the importance of deepening Africa's bond markets (for example by promoting the use of infrastructure bonds for the long-term financing of infrastructure development) as part of the domestic resource mobilization efforts of African countries (United Nations Economic Commission for Africa and New Partnership for Africa's Development, 2014). The most recent debates on Africa's infrastructure gap do not consider the role of domestic finance in financing infrastructure partly because accurate figures on government expenditures on infrastructure are difficult to obtain, and also because most Governments do not have a single or unified strategy for domestic infrastructure financing (Gutman et al., 2015).

A key message in this report is that African countries should harness the potential of domestic financial and bond markets as a source of alternative development finance for achieving their challenging development goals. As noted by the planning and coordinating agency of the New Partnership for Africa's Development in its strategic plan for 2014–2017, there is scope for improving domestic resource mobilization at all levels. However, domestic resource mobilization is not a panacea for Africa. African countries need a mix of development finance options, including debt. They cannot engage in domestic resource mobilization to finance their development needs without a corresponding formulation and implementation of policies aimed at financial deepening, inclusion and development, which includes the use and development of domestic debt instruments (UNCTAD, 2009; Mavrotas, 2008).

Given the complexity of Africa's development challenges, scale of its development finance needs and severity of its capacity constraints, domestic resource mobilization on its own cannot resolve all of Africa's financial needs. In addition to fiscal resources and domestic savings, it is optimal, and inevitable, that African countries leverage alternative sources of finance. Traditionally, official development assistance has played a critical role in the provision of financing for development in Africa. However, official development assistance in Africa has been falling as a share of total external flows (from 39.4 per cent in 2000 to 27.6 per cent in 2013) and traditional Development Assistance Committee donor countries have scaled back such assistance in real terms, especially in the least developed countries, most of which are in Africa (UNCTAD, 2015a). Only 5 of the 28 countries consistently meet the recommendation of allocating 0.7 per cent of GNI to official development assistance. Such assistance is often unpredictable and volatile, imposing costs on African economies (Canavire-Bacarreza et al., 2015). In addition, Africa cannot build for the future based on official development assistance that is subject to donor conditionalities rather than its own development agenda. For these reasons, reducing dependency on aid is an expressed goal in Agenda 2063. However, it is likely that for a number of least developed countries in Africa, there may be no substitute for official development assistance. Emerging economies, such as Brazil, China and India, have expanded the financial resources they provide to developing countries, financing both government activities and private sector projects (Pigato and Tang, 2015). Africa needs significant financing to eliminate infrastructure gaps, build productive capacity and implement the Sustainable Development Goals.

CHAPTER **2**

EXTERNAL DEBT DYNAMICS AND DEBT SUSTAINABILITY IN AFRICA

This chapter focuses on external debt in Africa and on current debt sustainability issues. The first part presents some definitions of external debt and the second part presents some stylized facts on external debt, followed by an analysis of the main drivers behind external debt accumulation. The third part outlines the major determinants of debt sustainability and analyses current debt sustainability frameworks. The final part concludes with a summary of the main findings.

A. DEFINING AND CHARACTERIZING EXTERNAL DEBT

Total external debt, as defined by the International Monetary Fund (IMF) and World Bank, is debt owed to non-residents (figure 1). Total external debt is the sum of public, publicly guaranteed and private non-guaranteed long-term debt, short-term debt and the use of IMF credit. Short-term debt includes all debt with an original maturity of one year or less and interest in arrears on long-term debt (World Bank, 2015a). Public and publicly guaranteed debt, in contrast to private non-guaranteed debt, comprises the long-term external obligations of public debtors,

Figure 1. External debt and its components

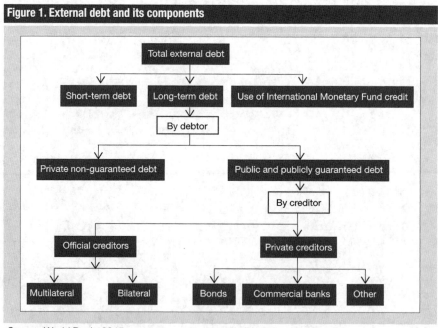

Source: World Bank, 2015a.

including national Governments, political subdivisions (or an agency of either) and autonomous public bodies, as well as the external obligations of private debtors that are guaranteed for repayment by a public entity (World Bank, 2015a). Public domestic debt, in contrast, refers to obligations of the same public entities but to lenders within a country. While recognizing that private debt may create public debt issues when private debt holders become unable to service their debt, this report primarily considers public (domestic and external) debt and public and publicly guaranteed debt, and does not focus on (non-guaranteed) corporate external debt.[6]

The definition of external and thus domestic debt may be debated. This report adopts a definition based on the residence of the creditor, in accordance with international organization best practices, such as those of UNCTAD, IMF and the World Bank. External debt is thus defined as debt owed to non-residents or based on the place of issuance and the legislation that regulates the debt contract whenever it is issued in foreign countries and under the jurisdiction of a foreign court.

Blurring the distinction between domestic and external debt

As UNCTAD (2015b) notes, the distinction between domestic and external debt is becoming blurred as there has been a shift in debt instruments since the early 1990s away from loans in foreign currency held by non-residents towards bonds that may be denominated in a foreign currency but held by residents. For example, foreign presences in domestic bond, equity and property markets are rising rapidly in developing countries, making it more difficult to distinguish domestic from external debt (Akyüz, 2014). A significant share of debt may be considered external under some criteria and domestic under others (UNCTAD, 2015b). Panizza (2008) states that the traditional dichotomy between domestic and external debt does not make sense in a world increasingly characterized by financial integration and open capital accounts. First, it is becoming increasingly difficult for countries to track the residences of the ultimate holders of their bonded debt. Second, while debt composition matters, the real sources of vulnerabilities in debt are currency and maturity mismatches. The division of domestic and external debt only makes sense if such a breakdown aids in tracking such vulnerabilities. Although a shift to domestic borrowing has important positive implications for debt management, policymakers should not be too complacent (Panizza, 2008). Countries should carefully balance one type of vulnerability (for example a currency mismatch) with another (maturity mismatch) when trading external debt for domestic debt.

In the African context, as regional integration gains momentum and flows of capital accelerate across national borders, the distinction between domestic and external debt will increasingly become blurred, as more and more institutional and private investors in Africa invest in bonds outside their countries but within the region, in bonds denominated in local currencies. Such increased cross-holding of domestic debt in Africa may have contagious effects across the continent owing to exposure to common global and regional shocks. For instance, an inability to repay or service debt by one country due to an external shock may affect the incomes of debt holders in other countries.

B. STYLIZED FACTS ON EXTERNAL DEBT

Scale of external debt

Rise of external debt levels

In 2011–2013, the annual average external debt stock of Africa amounted to $443 billion (22.0 per cent of GNI) compared with $303 billion (24.2 per cent of GNI) in 2006–2009. However, these broad trends in absolute terms do not reveal the rapid rise of external debt levels in several African countries in recent years.[7] Table 2 shows, for all 54 African countries, the level of external debt stock, external debt as a percentage of GNI and external debt as a percentage of exports of goods, services and primary income. As at December 2015, 30 African countries had qualified for debt relief under the Heavily Indebted Poor Countries Initiative and Multilateral Debt Relief Initiative. Three other countries (Eritrea, Somalia and the Sudan) are potentially eligible (box 2).

In 2011–2013, external debt to GNI ratios were less than 40 per cent in most African countries. For comparative purposes, external debt to GNI in the same period averaged 14.5 per cent in East Asia and the Pacific, 22.6 per cent in South Asia and 23.7 per cent in Latin America and the Caribbean. In the same period, external debt stock amounted to $132 billion (19.5 per cent of GNI) among heavily indebted poor countries, compared with $311 billion (31.3 per cent of GNI) among non-heavily indebted poor countries. Seychelles, a non-heavily indebted poor country, is an outlier in Africa, with an external debt–GNI ratio exceeding 200 per cent. With regard to external debt stock as a percentage of exports of goods, services and primary income, in the same period, the ratios ranged from 7.2 per cent in Algeria, a non-heavily indebted poor country, to 596.8 per cent in Sao Tome and Principe, a heavily indebted poor country.

Box 2. Heavily Indebted Poor Countries Initiative and Multilateral Debt Relief Initiative

Heavily Indebted Poor Countries Initiative: IMF and the World Bank launched this Initiative in 1996 as the first comprehensive approach to reducing the external debt of the world's poorest, most heavily indebted countries, with debt relief placed within an overall framework of poverty reduction. This Initiative only applies to eligible debt acquired during a specific period of time from specific creditors. A package of debt relief is identified for those countries whose debt burden is assessed by IMF and the World Bank as unsustainable after the full use of traditional debt relief mechanisms, known as the decision point. While full debt relief under the Initiative is provided at the completion point, some creditors may provide debt relief in the interim (the period between the decision point and the floating completion point). Under the enhanced framework, the completion point is floating as it is tied to the implementation of key structural reforms and poverty reduction policies.

Multilateral Debt Relief Initiative: At their annual summit in 2005, the Group of Eight leading industrial countries backed a proposal to cancel 100 per cent of the outstanding obligations of heavily indebted poor countries to the African Development Fund, IMF and the International Development Association. The proposal was subsequently endorsed by the Development Committee at the joint annual meeting of IMF and the World Bank in September 2005, as well as by the African Development Bank, and became known as the Multilateral Debt Relief Initiative. Heavily indebted poor countries need to reach the completion point under the enhanced framework of the Heavily Indebted Poor Countries Initiative in order to be eligible for the Multilateral Debt Relief Initiative. The implementation approach and the country coverage vary slightly across creditor institutions. However, all three institutions cover the outstanding debt as of 31 December 2004, after taking debt relief under the Heavily Indebted Poor Countries Initiative into account.

With 36 countries (30 in Africa) having reached the completion point under the latter and thus also receiving debt relief under the Multilateral Debt Relief Initiative, these two Initiatives are nearly complete. Only three countries (Eritrea, Somalia and the Sudan) may be considered for future debt relief under the Heavily Indebted Poor Countries Initiative.

External debt stock

On average, Africa's external debt stock grew rapidly, by 10.2 per cent per year in 2011–2013, compared with 7.8 per cent per year in 2006–2009. The annual average growth rate of Africa's external debt stock exceeded 10 per cent in eight heavily indebted poor countries and 13 non-heavily indebted poor countries. In 2011–2013, the external debt stock grew most rapidly in Mozambique (by, on average, 30 per cent per year), Cameroon (26 per cent per year) and Gabon, Nigeria, Rwanda and Seychelles (24 per cent per year each). These trends were driven to some extent by push and pull factors, such as the recent sharp decline in commodity prices[8] and resulting lower revenues (pull), and the global financial crisis. This led to greater risk taking behaviour (push), contributing to greater investor interest in emerging markets. Investors seeking better yields in Africa, given slow growth in advanced countries and higher rates of return based on the perceived risk of investing in Africa, have opened up new sources of external finance, often without the imposition of conditionalities, that African countries have taken advantage of. Currently, many African economies are entering a period of tightened borrowing conditions amid global concerns about emerging market growth prospects and financial volatility (IMF, 2015a). In general, external debt levels are now at relatively low levels in most African countries, aided by strong economic growth, low interest rates and the provision of comprehensive external debt relief to some 30 African countries under the Heavily Indebted Poor Countries Initiative and Multilateral Debt Relief Initiative. As at 2015, the two Initiatives had managed to substantially reduce the debt burdens of eligible countries.

Long-term debt sustainability, and debt ratios

Notwithstanding the decline in debt burdens through debt relief, long-term debt sustainability remains a challenge for many heavily indebted poor countries, with a few examples of debt ratios increasing rapidly in recent years (table 2). With regard to external debt as a percentage of GNI, several African countries[9] have experienced an upward trend, as shown in comparing the average in 2006–2009 with the average in 2011–2013, including for 12 heavily indebted poor countries (Burkina Faso, Rwanda, Mali, Uganda, Malawi, Senegal, Ghana, the United Republic of Tanzania, Benin, Ethiopia, the Niger and Mauritania, in order of increase in the external debt to GNI ratio) and seven non-heavily indebted poor countries (Botswana, Cabo Verde, Kenya, Mauritius, Morocco, Seychelles and South Africa). However, comparing the average in 2006–2009 with that in 2011–2013 may be misleading in terms of assessing debt accumulation following debt relief, as most heavily indebted poor countries in Africa received debt relief under the Multilateral Debt Relief Initiative in 2006 and 2007. Therefore, it is important to also compare the average in 2008–2010 with that in 2011–2013, which shows that debt ratios are also increasing (in descending order of absolute increase) in Sierra Leone and Cameroon. In addition, two countries are currently considered in debt distress, namely the Sudan and Zimbabwe, and seven countries are classified as high risk, namely Burundi, the Central African Republic, Chad, Djibouti, Ghana, Mauritania, and Sao Tome and Principe (table 3). In eight countries (Benin, Ghana, Malawi, Mozambique, the Niger, Sao Tome and Principe, Senegal and Uganda), a third of the gain in debt stock ratios since debt relief under the Heavily Indebted Poor Countries Initiative and Multilateral Debt Relief Initiative has been eroded over about four years since the completion point (Lewis, 2013; World Bank and Debt

Management Facility, 2013). If these rates of new borrowing persist, these countries may return to pre-relief debt to GDP ratios within a decade, regardless of improved economic growth.

Changing composition of debt: Concessional borrowing

Declining share of concessional debt in total external debt

The rapid rise in external borrowing by African countries is characterized by a marked change in concessionality and changes in the composition of debt. The share of concessional debt (defined as loans with an original grant element of 25 per cent or more) in total external debt in most African countries is declining; such debt declined in more than half of the 33 heavily indebted poor countries in Africa from 2006–2009 to 2011–2013 (figure 2b). This downward trend was also experienced by most non-heavily indebted poor countries in Africa, with only a few (Djibouti, Gabon, Nigeria, Swaziland and Tunisia) experiencing an increase between these two periods. This trend reflects the rising number of African countries reaching middle-income status, with implications for the composition of external financing.[10]

The concessional share of total external debt was less than 50 per cent on average in 2011–2013 in only seven of the heavily indebted poor countries in Africa (figure 2b), namely Côte d'Ivoire (27 per cent), Zambia (39 per cent), the Sudan (40 per cent), Liberia (40 per cent), the Central African Republic (43 per cent), Ghana (45 per cent) and the Democratic Republic of the Congo (48 per cent). In contrast, this concessional share was less than 50 per cent for 11 of the 16 non-heavily indebted poor countries for which data was available as at December 2015 (figure 2a).[11] Overall, the weighted share of concessional debt in total external debt in Africa fell from 42.4 per cent in 2006–2009 to 36.8 per cent in 2011–2013.

Rise of non-concessional debt

The rise in non-concessional financing (figure 6a) has been partly attributed to more flexible guidelines on external debt limits that were introduced in IMF-supported programmes, whereby low-income countries may take on more debt to support investment in high-return macrocritical infrastructure (Prizzon and Mustapha, 2014). A shift of most of Africa's debt from concessional to non-concessional sources, including bilateral and commercial creditors as well as international bond markets, is a concern for low-income countries; rescheduling government debts or borrowing more from commercial lenders than from multilateral lenders is generally much more difficult.

Table 2. Gross national income and external debt stocks, 2006–2009 and 2011–2013

	Gross national income (Millions of current dollars)		External debt stocks: Total (Millions of current dollars)		External debt stocks: Annual average rate of growth (Percentage)		External debt stocks (Percentage of gross national income)		External debt stocks (Percentage of exports of goods, services and primary income)	
	2006–2009	2011–2013	2006–2009	2011–2013	2006–2009	2011–2013	2006–2009	2011–2013	2006–2009	2011–2013
Non-heavily indebted poor countries										
Algeria	137 876	201 822	6 424	5 590	7.2	-7.0	4.7	2.8	10.1	7.2
Angola	56 650	102 836	13 585	21 136	20.8	11.5	24.3	20.7	30.2	30.1
Botswana	9 974	15 086	739	2 438	56.6	0.7	7.5	16.5	16.3	33.5
Cabo Verde	1 489	1 747	614	1 257	11.1	19.5	42.0	70.4	103.1	153.2
Djibouti	..	..	781	805	15.0	3.6	..	..	209.6	167.6
Egypt	148 246	250 291	33 381	39 859	3.9	12.4	23.0	15.9	71.2	78.1
Equatorial Guinea	8 824	11 463	..	..	..	..	..	..	..	..
Gabon	11 093	15 300	3 385	3 328	-22.8	24.2	34.0	19.9	..	..
Kenya	32 602	48 949	7 600	11 776	8.0	14.4	27.6	29.9	104.5	109.5
Lesotho	2 009	2 950	697	848	4.6	5.4	34.7	29.8	44.3	51.2
Libya	68 919	59 902	..	..	..	..	..	..	..	..
Mauritius	8 308	11 568	1 080	10 238	43.2	6.8	12.9	88.4	22.4	133.1
Morocco	78 719	96 616	21 061	34 326	10.2	14.6	26.9	35.4	84.3	104.3
Namibia	8 384	12 474	..	..	..	..	..	..	..	..
Nigeria	160 805	440 006	4 630	10 938	18.3	24.0	2.9	2.5	6.9	11.0
Seychelles	916	1 130	1 429	2 172	14.9	23.5	159.8	201.3	164.4	218.1
South Africa	280 822	383 007	71 068	133 612	9.6	9.7	26.4	36.3	77.9	110.4
South Sudan	9 915	10 728	..	..	..	..	..	..	..	..
Swaziland	3 035	3 393	455	533	5.1	-15.8	15.0	14.3	21.3	22.6
Tunisia	38 306	43 869	20 814	24 577	6.4	6.8	54.5	54.9	102.8	108.4
Zimbabwe	5 662	11 345	5 582	8 052	6.2	5.9	107.8	72.5	..	..
Heavily indebted poor countries										
Benin	5 838	7 672	929	2 096	26.7	12.5	15.7	27.3	67.2	105.1
Burkina Faso	7 322	10 714	1 524	2 458	18.0	5.8	20.8	22.9	163.5	75.5
Burundi	1 486	2 505	1 195	651	-21.8	6.3	83.7	25.5	1,048.2	272.3
Cameroon	20 952	27 086	3 142	3 928	-2.5	25.8	15.4	14.6	53.9	50.0
Central African Republic	1 769	1 979	887	558	-17.6	2.4	51.7	29.3	..	..
Chad	7 802	12 089	1 819	2 182	1.6	1.2	20.9	17.7	..	..
Comoros	478	591	285	225	0.0	-27.4	59.8	36.7	382.9	268.9
Congo	6 657	10 768	5 596	2 973	-8.3	14.4	88.9	27.0	95.5	..
Cote d'Ivoire	20 824	26 818	12 593	10 930	2.8	-4.3	63.8	43.4	117.0	88.9
Dem. Republic of the Congo	16 227	25 208	12 309	5 734	4.2	4.9	76.3	22.7	242.2	56.4
Eritrea	1 431	3 020	942	998	8.8	-5.3	66.7	33.7	..	..

Table 2 (contd.)

	Gross national income (Millions of current dollars)		External debt stocks: Total (Millions of current dollars)		External debt stocks: Annual average rate of growth (Percentage)		External debt stocks (Percentage of gross national income)		External debt stocks (Percentage of exports of goods, services and primary income)	
	2006–2009	2011–2013	2006–2009	2011–2013	2006–2009	2011–2013	2006–2009	2011–2013	2006–2009	2011–2013
Ethiopia	23 612	40 839	3 265	10 541	29.3	20.8	14.1	26.3	108.2	161.0
Gambia	804	873	574	504	-15.4	4.8	75.5	57.3	223.2	149.2
Ghana	24 799	41 792	5 410	13 227	23.6	18.5	21.6	31.7	81.7	82.4
Guinea	3 614	5 213	3 161	1 811	-0.2	-38.2	91.6	36.6	255.4	105.8
Guinea-Bissau	736	1 002	1 096	280	2.9	-1.1	153.4	31.9	865.0	137.0
Liberia	684	1 549	3 245	492	-23.1	9.9	553.6	31.1	572.8	55.2
Madagascar	7 635	9 877	2 268	2 838	20.9	1.4	29.8	28.7	105.6	140.9
Malawi	3 983	4 446	970	1 360	10.1	13.7	24.7	32.5	97.6	84.0
Mali	7 411	10 227	1 933	3 137	11.0	8.2	26.2	31.1	88.4	94.7
Mauritania	3 491	4 828	1 910	3 263	12.4	11.6	58.3	84.2	111.6	109.2
Mozambique	8 981	14 522	3 367	5 286	14.1	29.8	41.5	37.4	111.0	107.9
Niger	4 671	6 889	1 023	2 404	14.1	8.9	22.0	35.4	112.1	157.0
Rwanda	4 219	6 954	648	1 354	24.7	23.8	15.5	19.5	117.5	126.9
Sao Tome and Principe	167	272	202	216	-22.9	-3.6	129.6	80.0	952.6	596.8
Senegal	11 608	14 248	2 774	4 817	22.8	9.9	23.7	33.5	87.0	110.0
Sierra Leone	2 370	3 665	885	1 190	-14.3	15.2	40.3	32.8	257.9	112.7
Somalia	..	..	2 960	3 054	1.9	0.0	..	..	..	..
Sudan	44 079	62 847	19 901	21 785	4.3	3.0	46.6	40.4	230.9	297.9
Togo	2 564	3 408	1 785	762	-2.9	19.8	70.6	22.3	169.6	30.3
Uganda	13 109	21 889	1 978	3 800	30.0	15.6	15.4	20.6	71.7	78.1
United Republic of Tanzania	23 194	37 444	5 697	11 515	22.6	14.5	31.2	41.2	121.3	138.1
Zambia	13 881	24 283	3 022	5 308	15.8	6.4	26.8	26.6	64.2	53.1
Africa	1 363 994	2 170 000	302 620	443 165	7.8	10.2	24.2	22.0	71.7	70.6
Low-income developing economies	176 619	269 673	65 003	78 362	6.3	9.9	36.7	29.4	135.6	100.7
Middle-income developing economies	595 609	1 085 739	139 907	186 288	6.7	10.9	24.2	18.1	72.4	66.2
High-income developing economies	591 765	814 589	97 710	178 515	10.4	9.5	20.0	25.1	51.7	68.4
Non-heavily indebted poor countries	1 072 554	1 724 482	193 326	311 485	8.8	10.8	37.6	31.3	53.6	57.6
Heavily indebted poor countries	291 440	445 518	109 294	131 680	6.1	8.8	20.2	19.5	135.1	125.7

Source: World Bank, 2016b (accessed November 2015).

Notes: In this report, unless otherwise stated, heavily indebted poor countries are those that have qualified for, are eligible or potentially eligible and may wish to receive assistance under the Heavily Indebted Poor Countries Initiative as of September 2015.

The figures for the last six categories are weighted averages, whereby GNI in millions of current dollars is used as the weight.

Table 3. Risk of debt distress as at November 2015			
Low risk (10)	**Moderate risk (20)**	**High risk (7)**	**In debt distress (2)**
Benin	Angola	Burundi	Sudan
Ethiopia	Burkina Faso	Central African Republic	Zimbabwe
Kenya	Cabo Verde	Chad	
Liberia	Cameroon	Djibouti	
Madagascar	Comoros	Ghana	
Nigeria	Congo	Mauritania	
Rwanda	Côte d'Ivoire	Sao Tome and Principe	
Senegal	Democratic Rep.		
United Republic of	of the Congo		
Tanzania	Gambia		
Uganda	Guinea		
	Guinea-Bissau		
	Lesotho		
	Malawi		
	Mali		
	Mozambique		
	Niger		
	Sierra Leone		
	South Sudan		
	Togo		
	Zambia		

Source: IMF, 2015a, updated November 2015 with available IMF country reports and debt
        sustainability analyses.

Notes: There is no rating available for Algeria, Botswana, Egypt, Equatorial Guinea, Eritrea,
        Gabon, Libya, Mauritius, Morocco, Namibia, Seychelles, Somalia, South Africa,
        Swaziland or Tunisia. The classification of the risk of external public debt distress is as
        follows:
  • Low risk, when all the debt burden indicators are well below the thresholds
  • Moderate risk, when debt burden indicators are below the thresholds in the baseline
    scenario, but stress tests indicate that thresholds may be breached if there are external
    shocks or abrupt changes in macroeconomic policies
  • High risk, when the baseline scenario and stress tests indicate a protracted breach of
    debt or debt-service thresholds, but the country does not currently face any repayment
    difficulties
  • In debt distress, when the country is already having repayment difficulties

Nevertheless, many African countries are seeking to exploit opportunities to finance public investment and are increasingly relying on borrowing on non-concessional terms (Prizzon and Mustapha, 2014). Since 2007, several heavily indebted poor countries have issued sovereign bonds denominated in dollars in international capital markets. Te Velde (2014) estimates that bonds issued in sub-Saharan Africa in 2013 ($5.1 billion) were equivalent to 20 per cent of bilateral aid and 12 per cent of foreign direct investment in the region.

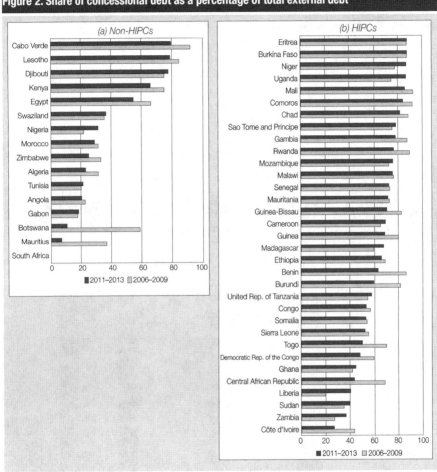

Figure 2. Share of concessional debt as a percentage of total external debt

Source: UNCTAD secretariat calculations, based on World Bank, 2016b (accessed December 2015).

Note: There is no available data for the following non-HIPCs: Equatorial Guinea, Libya, Namibia, South Sudan and Seychelles.

Prior to 2009, few African countries issued sovereign bonds; in 2010–2012 issuances rose moderately, with $1.5 billion–$2.5 billion issued annually. By 2014, issuances in Africa had risen to $6.25 billion (figure 3). The total stock of international sovereign bonds rose from $1 billion in 2008 to over $18 billion by 2014 (IMF, 2014a). At least 14 countries have issued international sovereign bonds (figure 4).

The average tranche is $1 billion, and the average maturity is 10 years and the average yield is 5–10 per cent (Tyson, 2015). Loans from the International Bank for Reconstruction and Development have a much longer maturity (up to 20 years) and their interest rates are much lower (a six-month London Interbank Offered Rate, plus either a fixed, variable or minimum 2 per cent spread, depending on the type of instrument). While the number of African countries issuing sovereign bonds has risen since 2010, especially among former heavily indebted poor countries (such as Côte d'Ivoire, Ethiopia, Ghana, the United Republic of Tanzania, Senegal and Zambia), Uganda is a notable exception to this trend.[12]

Ministries of Finance in Africa decided to place bonds in international financial markets for several reasons. First, although they are more expensive than most other financing options, notably non-concessional financing from multilateral

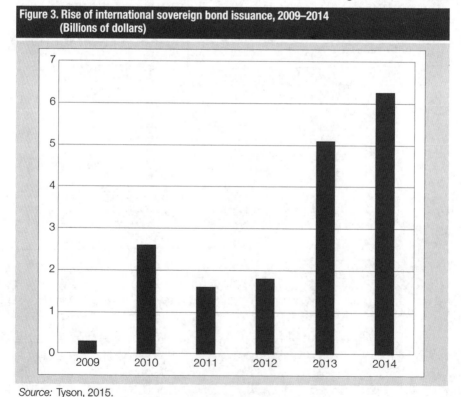

Figure 3. Rise of international sovereign bond issuance, 2009–2014 (Billions of dollars)

Source: Tyson, 2015.
Note: Data for 2014 cover only up to the third quarter.

development banks, their terms and conditions are usually more favourable than domestic bonds (IMF et al., 2013); international bonds often come with few conditionalities. Second, international sovereign bond issuance can provide a benchmark for pricing corporate bonds in international markets, over time expanding the yield curve,[13] and can help increase access by the private sector and State-owned enterprises (Prizzon and Mustapha, 2014). Third, the average size of international sovereign bonds, at $1 billion, is much larger than any other external flow to Governments, helping address the financing of infrastructure. Fourth, and more recently, international sovereign bonds have been issued to compensate for commodity earning downturns and maintain consumption levels.

Figure 4. International sovereign bond issuance since 2009, by issuance amount (Billions of dollars)

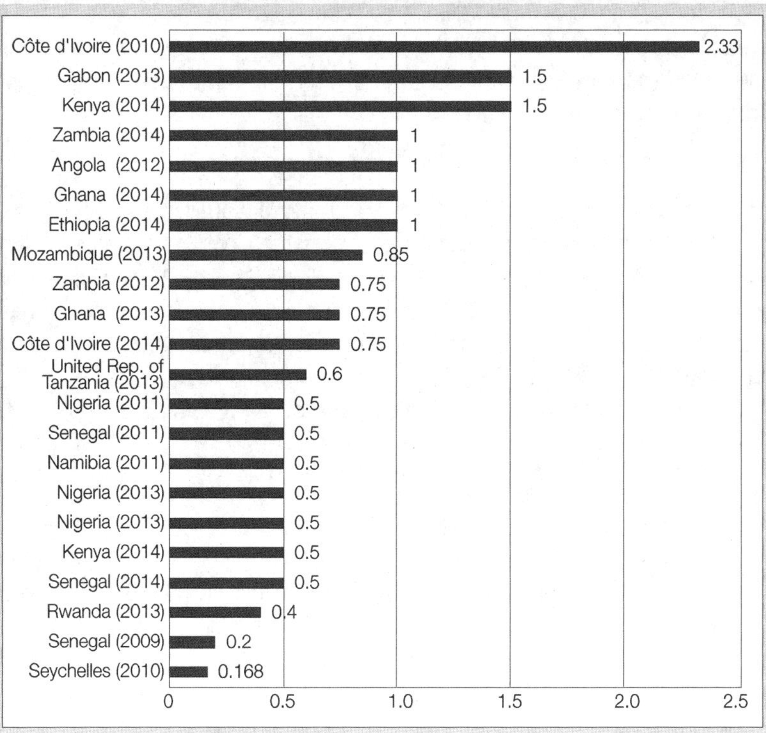

Country (year)	Amount
Côte d'Ivoire (2010)	2.33
Gabon (2013)	1.5
Kenya (2014)	1.5
Zambia (2014)	1
Angola (2012)	1
Ghana (2014)	1
Ethiopia (2014)	1
Mozambique (2013)	0.85
Zambia (2012)	0.75
Ghana (2013)	0.75
Côte d'Ivoire (2014)	0.75
United Rep. of Tanzania (2013)	0.6
Nigeria (2011)	0.5
Senegal (2011)	0.5
Namibia (2011)	0.5
Nigeria (2013)	0.5
Nigeria (2013)	0.5
Kenya (2014)	0.5
Senegal (2014)	0.5
Rwanda (2013)	0.4
Senegal (2009)	0.2
Seychelles (2010)	0.168

Source: Tyson, 2015.
Note: Data for 2014 cover only up to the third quarter.

Servicing international sovereign bonds, however, poses challenges and risks for prudent debt management, including interest rate and foreign exchange risks, as well as complex debt restructuring processes. For example, until recently, oversubscribed international sovereign bonds in Africa relied on prevailing low interest rates in international financial markets that increased investor interest in such instruments. If international interest rates rise, debt rollover[14] may not be as feasible in the future, and investor interest may shift to other instruments and markets (Sy, 2013). For example, in 2013, Ghana issued a bond denominated in foreign currency, with a coupon rate of 7.8 per cent. Interest rates on domestic debt are much higher at, on average, 19–23 per cent (box 3). However, if exchange rate devaluation (roughly 14 per cent per year since 2007) is taken into account, the nominal difference between the two rates (domestic debt and bonds denominated in foreign currency) is much narrower (te Velde, 2014). Similarly, international sovereign bonds may be more difficult to restructure than bank loans as, since they are open to investors and investment banks, there is a much larger number of creditors involved that must coordinate in the event of default, and the introduction of collective action clauses may be required.

Composition of public and publicly guaranteed debt

The share of private creditors in public and publicly guaranteed debt has been rising among both heavily indebted poor countries and non-heavily indebted poor countries. Public and publicly guaranteed debt on the creditor side may be broken down into debt from official creditors (multilateral loans from international organizations and bilateral loans from Governments) and debt from private creditors (publicly issued or privately placed bonds, commercial bank loans from private banks and other private financial institutions and other private creditors), as shown in figure 1.

Figures 6a and b show the breakdown of public and publicly guaranteed debt by creditor category in 2005–2013. Public and publicly guaranteed debt from private creditors not only rose in absolute terms in both heavily indebted poor countries (from $9 billion in 2005 to $20 billion in 2013) and non-heavily indebted poor countries (from $43 billion in 2005 to $91 billion in 2013) but also became more diversified. The share of the public and publicly guaranteed debt of private creditors has been increasing since 2005, from 8 per cent to 18 per cent of the total external debt stock of heavily indebted poor countries in Africa and from 31 per cent to 44 per cent of that of non-heavily indebted poor countries. Overall in Africa, the weighted share of private creditors in public and publicly guaranteed debt rose

Box 3. International sovereign bond issuance in Ghana

Following Seychelles and South Africa, Ghana was the third country in Africa to turn to international markets to finance its deficit. In 2007, Ghana launched a $750 million Eurobond with an interest rate of 8.5 per cent. In July 2013, Ghana issued another $1 billion Eurobond with an interest rate of 8.0 per cent, and in September 2014, issued another $1 billion Eurobond with an interest rate of 8.125 per cent (and a 12-year maturity). In October 2014, Standard and Poor's (2014) ratings services lowered its long-term foreign and local currency sovereign credit rating for Ghana from B to B-. However, in October 2015, Ghana issued another $1 billion Eurobond with an interest rate of 10.75 per cent (and a 15-year maturity), which was 100 per cent oversubscribed after the World Bank provided a partial bond guarantee of $400 million.

Comparing these Eurobonds with Ghana's traditional concessional external borrowing at far lower interest rates shows that these bonds constitute a significant change in the way Ghana finances its deficit. For example, while the debut Eurobond constituted 14.7 per cent of Ghana's total external debt outstanding in 2007, the 8.5 per cent interest payment on the bond constituted 39.1 per cent of Ghana's total interest payments on external debt in 2008. Figure 5a shows the sharp increase in external borrowing. Domestic borrowing also increased at about the same rate in 2011–2015. By 2015, the debt–GDP ratio had reached 71 per cent.

A considerable concern with regard to external (concessional and non-concessional) borrowing is currency depreciation, and Ghana's currency depreciated significantly. When Ghana launched its debut bond in 2007, the cedi was virtually at parity with the dollar (following redenomination of the cedi in 2007). As at October 2015, ¢1 was equivalent to only $0.026. In other words, the $750 million Eurobond, equivalent in 2007 to about ¢750 million, was in 2015 equivalent to a fiscal burden of about ¢3 billion.

Although Eurobonds come with far higher interest rates than traditional concessional borrowing instruments, their advantage is that they are still much cheaper in terms of interest rates than domestic borrowing. According to Standard and Poor's (2014), as at October 2014, the weighted average interest rates on the Government's cedi-denominated debt stood at 24 per cent per year for its 91-day treasury bills and at 23 per cent per year for its 182-day treasury bills. The high interest rate payments on domestic debt are shown in figure 5b.

In February 2015, Ghana reached an agreement with IMF for a $1 billion loan to bolster its faltering economy due to declining commodity (gold and cocoa) export prices, rising trade and fiscal deficits and rapidly escalating debt (Tafirenyika, 2015).

Figure 5. Ghana's external debt and interest payments to revenue

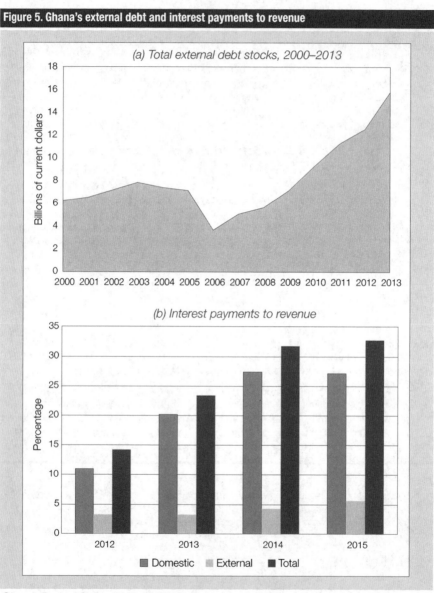

Sources: Bank of Ghana, 2015; UNCTAD secretariat calculations, based on Ghana Ministry of
         Finance, 2015.
Note: Data for 2015 is based on the revised 2015 budget as at October 2015.

from 17.6 per cent in 2006–2009 to 24.9 per cent in 2011–2013. Moreover, bonds have increased in importance for African non-heavily indebted poor countries, accounting for 44 per cent of debt from private creditors in 2005 and 73 per cent in 2013. However, this trend is largely driven by South Africa. Excluding South Africa, the bond share of private creditor debt increased from 30 per cent in 2005 to 48 per cent in 2013 in non-African heavily indebted poor countries. In heavily indebted poor countries in Africa, the share of private creditors in bonds increased from 24 per cent in 2005 to a high of 42 per cent in 2007, subsequently falling to a low of 16 per cent in 2011 and recovering to 25 per cent in 2013.

With regard to individual countries, the share of private creditors in public and publicly guaranteed debt exceeded 30 per cent in 2011–2013 in South Africa (the highest share, at 95 per cent, mostly in the form of bonds), followed by Gabon (63 per cent, mostly bonds), Angola (48 per cent, mostly commercial banks), the Congo (39 per cent, mostly bonds and commercial banks) and Ghana (32 per cent, mostly commercial banks). Seven countries, all heavily indebted poor countries, had no private creditors in their public and publicly guaranteed debt, namely Benin, the Comoros, Guinea-Bissau, Liberia, Mauritania, the Niger and Uganda.

Maturity and interest rates

Worsened terms and conditions of new borrowing for heavily indebted poor countries

Short-term debt (maturity of one year or less) as a percentage of total external debt remained low in most African countries in 2011–2013, ranging from 0 per cent in Lesotho and Nigeria (non-heavily indebted poor countries) and Burkina Faso and Senegal (heavily indebted poor countries) to more than 25 per cent in Benin, Somalia and Zimbabwe. However, the share of long-term public debt in total external debt fell in 31 countries (11 of which were non-heavily indebted poor countries) from 2006–2009 to 2011–2013. This indicates the rising significance of long-term private debt as a source of finance in African countries. The fall was most pronounced in Mauritius (from 75 to 14 per cent) followed by Algeria and Swaziland, among non-heavily indebted poor countries. Among heavily indebted poor countries, significant falls (by more than 20 per cent) occurred in Benin, Burundi, the Central African Republic and Togo. Heavily indebted poor countries in Africa have experienced on average a marked and steady decline in the maturity and grace period of new external debt commitments of public and publicly guaranteed debt since 2005.[15]

Figure 6. Public and publicly guaranteed debt in HIPCs and non-HIPCs, by creditor category, 2005–2013

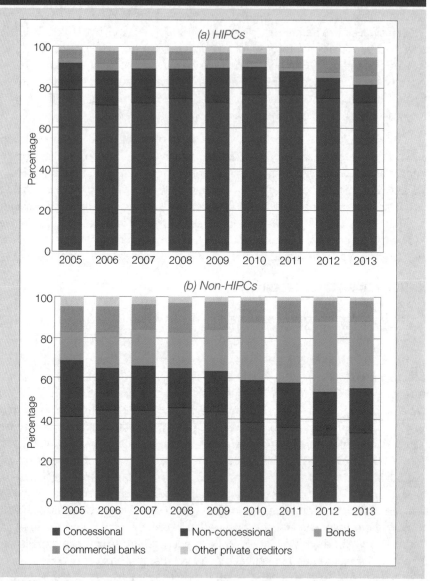

Source: World Bank, 2015a.

The average interest on new external debt (public and publicly guaranteed debt only) commitments of African heavily indebted poor countries has also worsened, although it remained below average for African non-heavily indebted poor countries and for low-income countries (figure 7c). This is to be expected given that the concessional share of borrowing is declining for heavily indebted poor countries. In addition, since 2007, several heavily indebted poor countries have ventured into international debt markets, facing interest rates far higher than the charges on International Development Association assistance. At the same time, interest rates for heavily indebted poor countries will be lower than those for non-heavily indebted

Figure 7. New external debt commitment averages

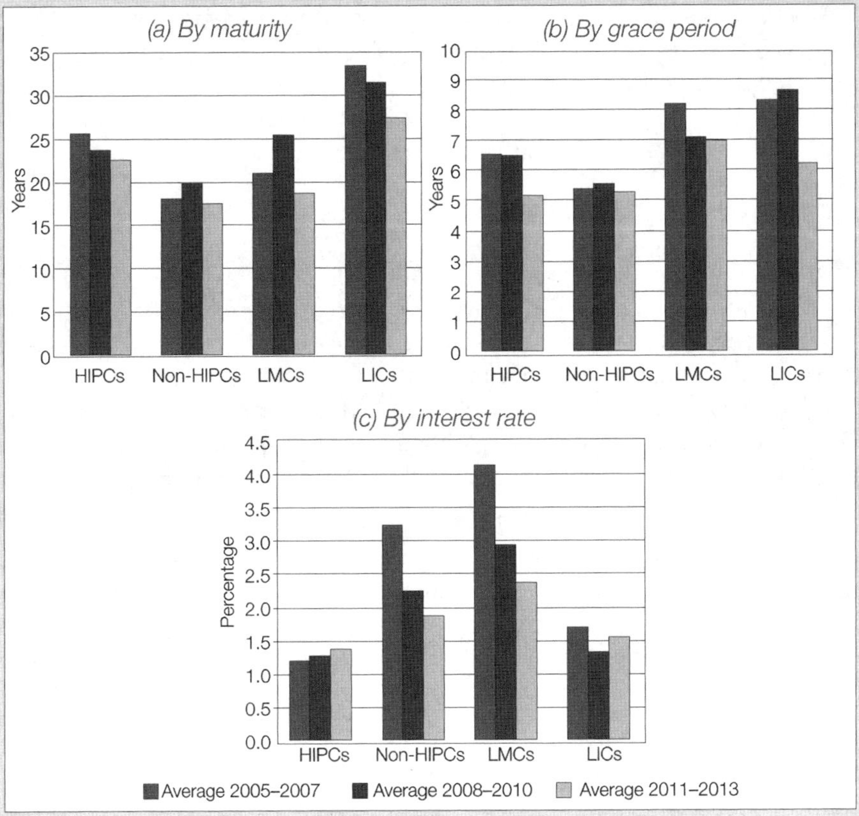

Source: World Bank, 2016b.
Note: Maturity and grace period are expressed in years.
Abbreviation: LIC, low-income country; LMC, lower middle-income country.

poor countries as the former continue to undertake more concessional borrowing than the latter. However, as shown in figures 7a and b, the change in maturity and grace period was marginal for non-heavily indebted poor countries, with both the maturity and grace period increasing in 2008–2010 before declining over the next three years. The interest rate, however, declined from 3.25 per cent in 2005–2007 to 1.87 per cent in 2011–2013 (figure 7c). This is to be expected, as global real interest rates worldwide have been declining substantially since the 1980s.

Increased share of external debt stock at a variable rate in total external (including non-guaranteed private) debt stock in some African non-heavily indebted poor countries

From 2006–2009 to 2011–2013, among non-heavily indebted poor countries, the share of external debt stock at a variable rate in total external debt stock rose by at least 10 percentage points in Angola, Botswana, Gabon, Egypt, Mauritius and Zimbabwe (table 4). Among heavily indebted poor countries, by this measure, only Ethiopia had an increase of at least 10 percentage points.

Currency composition of debt

Another indicator of interest linked to the exposure of African countries to potential debt-related risks is in the currency composition of public and publicly guaranteed debt. African countries hold debt in dollars, euros, Swiss francs, pounds sterling, yen and special drawing rights, as well as in a range of multiple currencies and in other currencies. The more debt stock held in a given foreign currency by an African country, the more vulnerable that country becomes to potential exchange rate and macroeconomic and political shocks in the foreign currency country.

In 2011–2013, only Swaziland and Zimbabwe held more than 20 per cent of their total external debt in multiple currencies other than dollars, euros, Swiss francs, pounds sterling, yen and special drawing rights and other currencies. A few countries (non-heavily indebted poor countries such as Botswana, Djibouti and South Africa and heavily indebted poor countries such as Benin, Burkina Faso, the Gambia, Guinea-Bissau, Mali, Mauritania and Togo) held at least 40 per cent of their total external debt in a range of other currencies. Countries that have significantly raised their debt exposure to a single currency from 2006–2009 to 2011–2013 (an increase of close to 20 per cent in the share of total external debt in the particular currency) include Cabo Verde and Sao Tome and Principe (shifting relatively more to euros) and the Congo, Liberia and Zambia (shifting relatively more to dollars).

The ratio of total reserves to total external debt stock can serve as an indicator of the ability of a country to respond either to adverse developments in debt markets, such as a sudden increase in debt interest payments due to a depreciation of the local currency relative to foreign currencies, or to any global shock, such as a fall in commodity prices, that affects debt service from export revenues. By this measure, countries with a ratio of less than 30 per cent include non-heavily indebted poor countries such as Mauritius (28 per cent) and Zimbabwe (7 per cent) and heavily indebted poor countries such as the Democratic Republic of the Congo (26 per cent), Eritrea (11 per cent), Guinea (9 per cent), Malawi (20 per cent), Mauritania (23 per cent), Sao Tome and Principe (26 per cent) and the Sudan (1 per cent). Maintaining adequate reserves to respond to an unexpected adverse development in debt and export trade markets should remain a priority for African countries as part of their policies to manage debt risks.

Persistent current account deficits may increase the probability of debt distress

A decomposition exercise conducted on the external debt–GDP ratio for 17 heavily indebted poor countries and 13 non-heavily indebted poor countries for which data were available (for 2005–2006, at the time of debt relief initiatives and for 2012–2013 (most recent)) shows that the external debt–GDP ratio declined by 14.9 percentage points on average in 2005–2006 and increased by 1.7 percentage points in 2012–2013 in all 30 countries. The latter increase may be broken down into a roughly 7.3 percentage point deficit on non-interest current accounts and a 0.5 percentage point interest payment, offset by GDP growth of 1.8 per cent and a residual of 4.3 per cent (the residual component captures the effects of all other factors, such as debt relief, and may be negative or positive). Similar results are also obtained if the analysis is repeated for only the 17 heavily indebted poor countries. While the external debt to GDP declined by 25.6 percentage points in 2005–2006, it increased slightly, by 0.7 percentage points, in 2012–2013, mainly due to the non-interest current account deficit (11.4 per cent).

Current account deficits have contributed to recent external debt dynamics in Africa, with balance of payments problems associated with rapid external debt accumulation in some instances (Battaile et al., 2015). This requires a careful monitoring of the debt vulnerabilities of countries to recent macrofiscal shocks such as falls in the prices of some commodities, especially oil, the slowdown in China and the sluggish recovery in Europe. According to Battaile et al. (2015), in

Table 4. Debt of African countries classified by maturity and other terms, 2006–2009 and 2011–2013

	Short-term debt (Percentage of total external debt)		Long-term public debt (Percentage of total external debt)		External debt stocks at variable rate (Percentage of total external debt)		Public and publicly guaranteed debt (Percentage of total external debt)		Total debt service (Percentage of exports of goods, services and primary income)	
	2006–2009	2011–2013	2006–2009	2011–2013	2006–2009	2011–2013	2006–2009	2011–2013	2006–2009	2011–2013
Non-heavily indebted poor countries										
Algeria	15.6	22.1	53.8	30.4	23.1	13.9	56.3	31.4	7.0	0.9
Angola	17.8	0.8	78.4	91.7	49.6	72.3	78.4	91.7	8.5	5.7
Botswana	8.7	17.0	88.8	77.2	20.4	69.9	88.8	77.2	1.0	1.4
Cabo Verde	0.2	0.1	97.1	98.4	11.6	13.2	97.1	98.4	5.3	4.7
Djibouti	17.0	12.2	79.8	81.4	0.8	4.4	79.8	81.4	8.3	8.5
Egypt	7.0	10.5	89.8	85.3	9.0	19.2	91.3	85.9	6.1	7.1
Equatorial Guinea	..	..	..	..	..	..	..	..	..	..
Gabon	7.3	5.6	89.3	87.3	10.3	26.5	89.3	87.3	5.9	5.1
Kenya	11.4	15.0	83.3	74.3	3.2	6.7	83.3	74.3	3.4	2.4
Lesotho	0.0	0.0	93.1	87.3	1.4	1.9	93.1	87.3	..	..
Libya	..	..	..	..	..	..	..	..	..	..
Mauritius	14.3	24.2	74.7	14.2	34.2	68.9	74.7	14.2	3.8	38.7
Morocco	8.9	12.9	76.5	73.5	35.7	32.9	76.9	73.7	15.0	12.0
Namibia	..	..	..	..	..	..	..	..	..	..
Nigeria	0.0	0.0	30.7	35.8	66.2	51.3	30.9	35.8	3.6	0.5
Seychelles	..	..	..	..	..	..	..	..	..	..
South Africa	32.8	18.8	29.3	37.8	44.9	43.9	29.3	37.8	6.5	6.7
South Sudan	..	..	..	..	..	..	..	..	..	..
Swaziland	10.2	20.1	84.3	65.6	20.3	14.4	84.3	65.6	2.2	1.8
Tunisia	19.7	24.0	68.5	64.5	28.0	29.0	68.9	65.8	11.6	11.6
Zimbabwe	29.8	29.8	64.9	48.4	10.2	22.9	64.9	48.4	..	..
Heavily indebted poor countries										
Benin	8.1	25.4	87.1	64.9	0.0	0.0	87.1	64.9	3.4	4.5
Burkina Faso	4.7	0.0	89.6	88.7	0.2	0.3	89.6	88.7	4.8	2.4
Burundi	1.5	1.9	83.5	60.0	0.0	0.0	83.5	60.0	16.9	8.9
Cameroon	5.9	5.2	70.2	73.4	22.1	14.1	70.2	73.4	7.8	3.4
Central African Republic	10.2	16.2	77.2	51.8	0.8	0.0	77.3	51.8	..	..
Chad	0.7	0.8	94.9	95.8	0.8	6.8	94.9	95.8	..	..
Comoros	4.2	1.5	93.0	84.3	0.0	2.1	93.0	84.3	17.5	5.7

Table 4 (contd.)

	Short-term debt (Percentage of total external debt)		Long-term public debt (Percentage of total external debt)		External debt stocks at variable rate (Percentage of total external debt)		Public and publicly guaranteed debt (Percentage of total external debt)		Total debt service (Percentage of exports of goods, services and primary income)	
	2006–2009	2011–2013	2006–2009	2011–2013	2006–2009	2011–2013	2006–2009	2011–2013	2006–2009	2011–2013
Congo	7.1	6.3	91.4	88.5	15.5	1.4	91.4	88.5	1.6	..
Democratic Rep. of the Congo	4.9	5.3	86.4	72.8	22.1	18.2	86.4	72.8	9.2	3.0
Côte d'Ivoire	7.2	2.8	83.9	66.5	33.7	39.2	83.9	66.5	6.3	6.8
Eritrea	1.8	2.1	95.7	95.5	2.9	3.9	95.7	95.5	..	..
Ethiopia	1.9	1.3	95.8	94.0	14.6	35.4	95.8	94.0	4.3	6.6
Gambia	4.6	2.3	88.9	79.8	2.9	5.9	88.9	79.8	9.7	7.5
Ghana	24.8	22.7	68.1	68.1	6.9	10.0	68.1	68.1	4.3	3.7
Guinea	3.8	4.4	92.5	82.3	5.1	5.5	92.5	82.3	13.0	8.3
Guinea-Bissau	12.7	11.9	85.9	76.6	1.4	0.0	85.9	76.6	8.0	2.2
Liberia	43.6	2.4	29.9	43.0	5.7	0.0	29.9	43.0	60.1	0.5
Madagascar	24.4	14.4	69.5	76.0	0.8	0.8	69.6	76.0	2.4	2.3
Malawi	7.3	1.4	81.6	78.3	0.0	0.0	81.6	78.3	4.7	2.2
Mali	0.9	3.3	95.2	88.8	2.5	3.7	95.2	88.8	3.3	2.4
Mauritania	13.1	5.7	84.6	88.0	8.3	3.9	84.6	88.0	5.3	4.8
Mozambique	17.4	4.5	76.2	88.5	1.2	0.8	76.2	88.5	1.3	1.8
Niger	12.5	5.8	78.4	87.4	1.8	1.3	78.4	87.4	9.1	2.4
Rwanda	2.0	5.6	90.2	84.8	0.0	0.0	90.2	84.8	3.9	2.5
Sao Tome and Principe	9.6	8.6	85.3	81.7	2.9	3.5	86.1	83.8	20.9	16.4
Senegal	6.0	0.0	81.0	85.2	14.1	6.3	81.0	85.2	6.1	8.4
Sierra Leone	1.3	6.6	84.9	69.8	0.3	0.1	84.9	69.8	3.6	2.1
Somalia	26.5	27.1	66.5	65.0	0.7	0.6	66.5	65.0	..	..
Sudan	32.4	24.9	64.8	72.1	11.4	19.8	64.8	72.1	4.4	5.5
Togo	9.5	5.7	86.0	60.2	7.4	0.0	86.0	60.2	6.2	1.4
Uganda	10.5	3.8	84.4	89.1	0.0	0.0	84.4	89.2	3.1	1.5
United Republic of Tanzania	21.4	15.7	61.3	66.1	19.5	18.9	61.3	66.1	2.1	1.9
Zambia	18.3	12.9	37.1	49.1	35.1	24.0	37.1	49.1	3.0	2.5

Source: World Bank, 2016b (accessed March 2016).

sub-Saharan Africa, debt relief (up to 2009) and foreign direct investment inflows were the main driving forces of debt reduction in the 2000s, while current account imbalances significantly contributed to debt increases throughout the 2000s. However, with regard to foreign direct investment, while inflows may contribute to reducing reliance on debt, increased net income payments associated with such inflows may also contribute to current account deficits that increase reliance on debt financing. Recent debt accumulation in several African countries appears to have been driven mainly by non-interest current account deficits, in both heavily indebted poor countries and non-heavily indebted poor countries. However, as previously noted, there are other potential drivers of debt accumulation in Africa, such as the end of the commodity super cycle and, in recent decades, faster integration into international financial markets, in particular following the global financial crisis.

In sum, recent debt accumulation in several African countries appears to be driven mainly by the deficit of non-interest current accounts, in both heavily indebted poor countries and non-heavily indebted poor countries. In general, improving current account deficits in developing countries with undiversified exports may take time, implying a need for structural transformation in the composition of exports and possibly also of imports. This, in turn, is a more complicated process than achieving a higher growth rate for a few years (Vaggi and Prizzon, 2014).

C. ACHIEVING AND MAINTAINING DEBT SUSTAINABILITY

As stated in UNCTAD (2015b), the structure and composition of debt matter for debt sustainability. Flassbeck and Panizza (2008) note, for instance, that different types of debt give way to different vulnerabilities and that discussions on debt sustainability should refer not only to external public debt but also encompass private debt. Debt sustainability exercises have traditionally focused on external debt since, until the early 1990s, most developing country debt was public and most public debt was external. However, recently, an increasing share of developing country debt has either been issued by private borrowers or been domestic in nature or both, as discussed in the African context in section B. Ideally, the various dimensions of debt should be considered and the risk level of each dimension assessed. The three main dimensions are maturity and currency characteristics, type of lender and type of borrower. With regard to the first, short-term debt and foreign currency debt tend to pose greater risks for borrowers than long-term domestic debt. While a foreign presence may play an important role, particularly in stock markets, bond markets are the most likely to be affected (Akyüz, 2014). With regard to the second, lending by official creditors poses less risk than lending by private creditors as such funding sources are more stable and less prone to financial contagion. With regard to the third, public debt poses greater risks than private debt due to its budgetary implications, although the latter can also present budgetary problems due to contingent liabilities (Flassbeck and Panizza, 2008). Through an empirical analysis of factors that may increase a country's probability of incurring a debt crisis, Flassbeck and Panizza (2008) find evidence that such a probability is higher with external public debt contracted from private creditors in foreign currency, lower with domestic public debt and lower still with external public debt from official creditors.[16] No conclusive results are reached with private debt. Ideally, debt sustainability exercises should take into account the risk levels of different components of debt.

Revisiting debt sustainability frameworks

In 2005, IMF and the World Bank introduced the joint World Bank–IMF Debt Sustainability Framework for Low-income Countries, in order to assist low-income countries[17] in achieving debt sustainability with regard to new borrowing from concessional official loans (World Bank and IMF, 2014). The Framework has the following three key objectives: to guide the borrowing decisions of low-income countries in a way that matches their financing needs with their current and prospective repayment ability, taking into account each country's circumstances; provide guidance for lending and grant allocation decisions of creditors to ensure that resources are provided to low-income countries on terms that are consistent with both progress towards their development goals and long-term debt sustainability; and help detect potential crises early so that preventive action can be taken. The Framework is currently undergoing what may become a substantial revision (World Bank and IMF, 2015). Within the Framework, debt sustainability analyses are regularly conducted and consist of the following:

- An analysis of a country's projected debt burden over the next 20 years and its vulnerability to external and policy shocks (baseline and shock scenarios are calculated);

- An assessment of the risk of debt distress in that time, based on indicative debt burden thresholds that depend on the quality of the country's policies and institutions (table 5);

- Recommendations for a borrowing (and lending) strategy that limits the risk of debt distress.

The Framework analyses both external and public sector debt. Given that loans to low-income countries vary considerably in their interest rates and lengths of repayment, the Framework focuses on the net present value of debt obligations in order to ensure comparability over time and across countries, although the use of short-term and currency-specific discount rates may distort such comparability. To assess debt sustainability, debt burden indicators are compared with indicative thresholds over a 20-year projection period. A debt burden indicator that exceeds its indicative threshold suggests a risk of experiencing some form of debt distress (table 3). The Framework classifies countries into one of three policy performance categories (weak, medium and strong) using the World Bank's country policy and institutional assessment index[18] and uses different indicative thresholds for debt burdens depending on the category (table 5).

Thresholds corresponding to strong policy performers according to the Framework are the highest, indicating that in countries with strong policies, debt accumulation poses less risk. Despite various improvements in debt sustainability frameworks and analyses since the 1990s, many still consider the Framework too mechanical and backward looking and excessively restrictive in not sufficiently differentiating between capital and recurrent public spending (UNCTAD, 2004). In many African countries, there remains a tension between accumulating external debt to finance national development strategies and the Sustainable Development Goals and maintaining external debt sustainability. For instance, to improve the current Framework, a limited increase in debt financing may need to be permitted for African countries to progress in achieving the Goals without creating a debt overhang.

Table 5. Debt burden thresholds in the World Bank–International Monetary Fund Debt Sustainability Framework

Policy performance	Net present value of debt as percentage of			Debt service as percentage of	
	Exports	Gross domestic product	Revenue	Exports	Revenue
Weak	100	30	200	15	18
Medium	150	40	250	20	20
Strong	200	50	300	25	22

Source: World Bank and IMF, 2014.

There have been concerns among African low-income countries that the Framework may lock low-income countries into a scenario of low debt and low growth. In particular, there is an inherent tension in most low-income countries between debt financing for national development strategies to achieve the Sustainable Development Goals and maintaining debt sustainability. Concern with regard to a scenario of low debt and low growth has been heightened by the emerging consensus among the main donors in the mid-2000s that countries that have received debt relief under the Multilateral Debt Relief Initiative should not accumulate new debt in the near future, even if their debt levels are below the thresholds of the new framework. However, restrictions on concessional financing have been a key factor for many African low-income countries in increasing domestic borrowing and, as previously noted, some African low-income countries have also started borrowing from non-concessional international capital markets.

Figure 8 shows a comparison of the debt burden thresholds and actual debt burden values of the average heavily indebted poor country in Africa in 2000–2013 in order to present the level of restrictiveness of debt burden thresholds. As there is a wide range of debt levels within the group of heavily indebted poor countries, the averages are not optimal, although they still provide some information. Figures 8c and e present data on debt service indicators. In the period under consideration, it is apparent that none of the averages ever surpassed the debt thresholds, not even in countries with weak policy performances. In contrast, figures 8a, b and c show that the average net present value debt indicators were mainly below the thresholds in countries with medium and strong policy performances. Finally, as shown in figures 8d and e, none of the averages came close to the threshold for weak policy performances, according to the Framework. This may indicate that the thresholds became less binding in the early 2010s, that is, heavily indebted poor countries were able to borrow more as they were below the debt thresholds. The rising debt indicators and the fact that some countries have more recently been categorized as having high levels of debt indicate that many of these countries have borrowed more aggressively in recent years. However, debt difficulties are not only driven by excessive borrowing; changes in exchange rates and terms of trade, as well as exogenous shocks, can all lead to sudden increases in debt ratios.

There may be a need to revisit current debt sustainability frameworks in light of the growing development finance requirements of African countries and developing countries generally, especially since the adoption of the Sustainable Development Goals. Clearly, the dilemma is how to achieve the Goals while maintaining debt

Figure 8. Comparison of debt burden thresholds and actual debt averages of African HIPCs (Percentage)

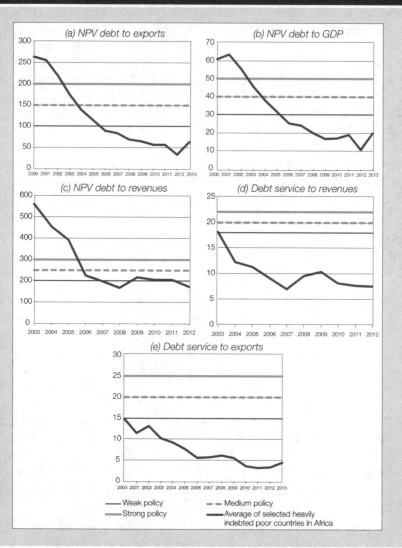

Source: UNCTAD secretariat calculations, based on World Bank, 2016c.
Note: The average net present value covers 2000–2013, except for revenue indicators, which
         cover 2003–2012.

sustainability and whether this may be achieved. More than a decade ago, the relevant report of the Secretary-General proposed to redefine debt sustainability as the level of debt that would allow a country to achieve the Millennium Development Goals and reach 2015 without an increase in debt ratios (United Nations, 2005). Today, with the adoption of the Sustainable Development Goals, there is a similar need to outline the Debt Sustainability Framework in a manner consistent with the Goals. There is also a need to clarify the purpose of the Framework in connection with the Goals (for example by including scenarios related to the Goals, based on funding for the Goals and the likely sources of finance). Some options for improving the current Framework to allow a limited increase in the debt financing of countries in order to allow for African countries to make progress in achieving the Goals without creating a debt overhang include the following:

- Make adjustments for investments related to the Goals: A revised Framework should have improved systems for monitoring the uses of debt, ensuring that countries are borrowing to finance productive investments rather than for consumption and in order to achieve the Goals;

- Place greater emphasis on payment caps on debt service: Refocusing debt sustainability for low-income countries on public debt service payments to government revenues and implementing payment caps on debt service payments for low-income countries, with a proportional reduction in debt service payments to all creditors, including commercial creditors, would be a significant improvement. Such debt service limits would have to be part of binding collective action clauses.[19] Given uncertainty regarding whether a debt problem reflects a temporary illiquidity or a more permanent debt overhang, debt service caps may be implemented on a temporary basis without reducing total debt stocks. If it becomes clear that a country faces a longer term debt overhang, a debt stock reduction would have to be implemented.

There is a case for reforming the current Framework for low-income countries, especially in the context of financing the Sustainable Development Goals and implementing national and regional development strategies in Africa. Aside from the problems and limitations previously mentioned, there are other more fundamental challenges concerning the country policy and institutional assessment index (Gunter, forthcoming) and the underlying modelling logic of the Framework (Guzman and Heymann, 2015). The Framework may be improved by addressing the following aspects:

- There is a need to strengthen the assessment of total public debt. At present there is no formal rating for total public debt, only external public debt, which is a particular challenge given the heterogeneity of low-income countries in Africa and the rising importance of domestic debt (chapter 3). There is also a need to better capture the risks of market access such as rollover risks, which are only partially reflected in debt service indicators, and the risks associated with public debt;

- There is a need for the Framework to better reflect risks from contingent liabilities (Guzman and Heymann, 2015).[20] The main challenge relates to the lack of available data and reliability, as well as limited experience with risks related to public–private partnerships (chapter 4). The Framework also needs to better capture risks from natural disasters, as low-income countries are often the most vulnerable to such disasters;

- There may be a need to recalibrate existing Framework models for macroeconomic projections of growth and debt dynamics in low-income countries that may systematically overestimate their capacities to repay debt (Guzman and Heymann, 2015). External debt thresholds centred on the country policy and institutional assessment index have been criticized for attempting to measure too many variables unrelated to a country's ability to repay debt (Ferrarini, 2008). There is also a lack of country-specific data in deriving thresholds, given that slight differences in country policy and institutional assessment index scores may lead to major threshold differences (Gunter, forthcoming).

Multilateral debt relief and workout mechanisms

The repayment of debt depends on growth and development in the debtor country, meaning that a country's debt sustainability should matter not only to the debtor but also to its creditors. If debt sustainability frameworks are an ex ante response to a rising accumulation of debt, then debt relief and workout mechanisms represent an ex post response to debt distress. IMF is currently considering ways of improving its lending policies for countries experiencing sovereign debt distress in order that the costs of crisis resolution may be minimized for debtors and creditors and, ultimately, the international financial system. The most recent proposal under consideration has the following two key elements: introduction of a debt reprofiling option, to make the IMF lending framework more flexible when the borrowing country's debt is assessed as sustainable but not with high probability; and elimination of the systemic exemption introduced in 2010[21] to allow the framework to give exceptional access even when debt sustainability is doubtful (IMF, 2014b). No decision has been made on the suggested reforms to date. Furthermore, recognizing the vulnerability of heavily indebted poor countries to natural and other shocks, IMF established a catastrophe containment and relief trust in February 2015 to provide grants for debt relief to the poorest and most vulnerable countries affected by catastrophic natural disasters or public health disasters, including epidemics, in order to make available resources to meet exceptional balance of payments needs created by such disasters, rather than having to assign such resources to debt service.[22] Three countries affected by the Ebola virus disease outbreak (Guinea, Liberia and Sierra Leone) received close to $100 million in assistance from this trust in February and March 2015.

The annual General Assembly resolution on external debt has repeatedly stressed the importance of promoting responsible sovereign lending and borrowing. As a first step in addressing this gap in the international financial architecture, in 2009, UNCTAD launched an initiative that sought to build consensus on a set of internationally agreed principles to promote responsible sovereign lending and borrowing, as transparent, fair, predictable, coordinated and legitimate lending would help to promote a durable and just solution to debt restructuring. The principles on promoting responsible sovereign lending and borrowing (UNCTAD, 2012a) are noted in the Addis Ababa Action Agenda and in General Assembly resolution 69/319 on basic principles on sovereign debt restructuring processes, adopted in September 2015.

D. ADDRESSING THE CHALLENGES OF RISING EXTERNAL DEBT TO ACHIEVE DEBT SUSTAINABILITY

In 2011–2013, the external debt stock of Africa amounted on average to $443 billion (21 per cent of GNI), compared with $303 billion (22.6 per cent of GNI) in 2006–2009. External debt to GNI ratios are low, at less than 40 per cent in most African countries. Nevertheless, these broad trends hide the rapid reaccumulation of external debt in several African countries in recent years. Notwithstanding the decline in debt burdens through debt relief, long-term debt sustainability remains a challenge for many heavily indebted poor countries, with a few instances of debt ratios increasing rapidly in recent years.

As previously noted, the rapid rise in external borrowing by countries in the region is characterized by a marked change in concessionality and changes in the composition of debt. The share of concessional debt in total external debt in African countries is falling. Given the rising share of non-concessional financing, African countries should strengthen their capacities to manage their debt sustainably, limit fungibility and enhance accountability and transparency in the uses of funds. Debt management performance assessment evaluations of 58 low-income countries undertaken in 2008–2014 by the World Bank found that the majority of countries did not meet the minimum requirements for sound practices in 7 of 15 debt performance indicators and noted that debt management capacities in low-income countries were generally inadequate, and particularly weak in heavily indebted poor countries (World Bank and IMF, 2015). As low-income countries in Africa move towards commercial funding and become more integrated into global capital markets, while liquidity buffers have narrowed, they need to enhance efforts to build their debt management capacities. In this regard, efforts undertaken by Nigeria are worth noting. Before renegotiating debt relief in 2005, Nigeria established a budget office and debt management office and also created a domestic debt rating agency (Adams, 2015). The creation of such institutional capacities for rating, monitoring and managing debt, whether public or private, may be emulated in other African countries. Given that a large part of external debt is used by Government a priori to finance development projects, attention should also be paid to strengthening skills and capacities in project planning, management and evaluation and the conduct of cost–benefit analyses to ascertain the profitability of public investment through such funds. Such efforts have been aiding Nigeria in managing its levels of debt more sustainably. The UNCTAD Debt Management and Financial Analysis System is an example of technical assistance aimed at strengthening government capacities in debt management in African countries (box 4).

Countries should empower public affairs and budget committees in State legislatures and national audit offices with oversight authority and ensure transparency and accountability. Parliamentarians, legislators and State auditors should also exercise vigorous oversight and demand transparency on debt terms and spending plans (Adams, 2015).

> **Box 4. Addressing capacity constraints in debt management and financial analysis**
>
> The UNCTAD Debt Management and Financial Analysis System provides debt management support in 23 African countries. For example, Uganda has improved its capacity to effectively manage its debt with the support of the System, which includes the provision of a specialized debt management and financial analysis software developed to meet the operational, statistical and analytical needs of debt managers in developing countries. Significant improvements have been achieved in the quality of the debt database in Uganda, as demonstrated by improved scores in 2015 under the public expenditure and financial accountability framework, contributing to improved transparency and accountability, debt reporting and debt sustainability analyses. In 2015, the Government published its first debt statistical bulletin, one of the main outcomes of the technical assistance and the implementation of the System's debt recording system. Uganda is now independently elaborating an annual debt sustainability analysis and, also in 2015, developed a new medium-term debt management strategy, both issued by the Ministry of Finance.

Whether domestic or external, the uses of debt matter for growth and debt sustainability

The ownership of debt, that is, whether it is owned by domestic or foreign residents, is significant. Domestic and external debt each has different macroeconomic implications, as highlighted in this chapter. However, whether debt is domestic or external, the uses to which such debt is put (whether towards consumption or productive investment) also affect debt sustainability. For instance, if debt is acquired to meet recurrent expenditures, this may lead to significant liabilities and debt sustainability challenges for the State, as for example in Mozambique (Financial Times, 2016) and Ghana (box 3). If debt is used to finance investment that contributes to building productive capacities and future increases in GDP, it ensures that countries may generate the resources needed to repay and service their debts. Using debt to finance investment for economic diversification purposes is even more important in ensuring that countries have the capacities to respond to unforeseen external shocks and muster the ability to repay their debts. In both the debt crises in Africa and Latin America in the 1980s, debt situations became unsustainable in the aftermath of an external shock (for African countries, a commodity bust, and for Latin America, the Volcker shock associated with hikes in United States of America interest rates induced by oil price rises) following a build-up of debt for consumption purposes.

CHAPTER **3**

DOMESTIC DEBT DYNAMICS IN AFRICA

A. INTRODUCTION

A key development over the past decade has been an increasing reliance on domestic debt markets by African Governments to expand their net borrowing, in most cases reflecting a need to fill the gap created by a decline in official development assistance as a share of total external flows. Achieving high and sustainable levels of investment needed for Africa's development will require a combination of foreign and domestic resources. This may increase ownership of the development agenda and enhance the effectiveness of strategies and the focus on sectors in which investment is most productive. At the same time, with domestic debt playing an increasingly important role, countries will face new risks as the numbers of creditors and debt instruments continue to expand, and domestic debt will become instrumental in assessing public debt sustainability owing to its size and swift growth.[23] This chapter addresses the following broad questions:

- What are the current trends and dynamics in public domestic debt in Africa?

- What are the current main domestic debt risk factors and how can such risks be best managed?

- What are the causal factors underlying rising domestic debt?

This chapter highlights the potential role of public domestic debt in Africa's development finance, the characteristics of public domestic debt in Africa and its evolution, marketable versus non-marketable domestic debt, public domestic debt by maturity and by holders and interest costs. This chapter also considers the dynamics of public domestic debt accumulation and the drivers of the growth in domestic debt. As there is still insufficient data readily available on Africa's domestic debt to allow for a comparison of a significant number of countries over an extended period of time, this analysis is limited to data on five countries, presenting detailed case studies of domestic debt in Ghana, Kenya, Nigeria, the United Republic of Tanzania and Zambia.

Defining public domestic debt

In line with the 2013 edition of the Public Sector Debt Statistics Guide for Compilers and Users and the basis on which African countries record and report their statistics, this report adopts the residency criteria to define domestic debt (chapter 2), which is analytically useful and relevant to the study of resource transfers between residents and non-residents (Panizza, 2008). However, it is difficult to apply in practice with respect to marketable debt instruments, as it requires periodic surveys to identify the ultimate debt holders. For the purposes of this report, residence status is determined at the time of issuance in the primary market. With regard to instruments and institutional coverage, the analysis is limited to the securitized domestic financial liabilities of the central Government in five countries, namely Ghana, Kenya, Nigeria, the United Republic of Tanzania and Zambia. Information on public domestic debt data is obtained from individual country reports, such as central bank annual reports, country debt office databases and IMF country reports.

B. THE RISE IN DOMESTIC DEBT

Domestic debt markets may have the potential to assume a more prominent role in funding the future development of some African countries.

First, as shown in figure 9a, Africa is among the world's fastest growing regions, with average GDP growth rates exceeding 4 per cent per year since 2000. Since 2007, only developing Asia has surpassed Africa's growth rates. However, given the contraction in commodity prices, coupled with subdued global demand, these growth rates may be difficult to maintain (World Bank and IMF, 2015). Economic growth in Africa has been accompanied by low and stable inflation, which in most countries has remained in the single digits. In addition, a growing number of countries have achieved middle-income status, with per capita annual incomes in excess of $1,000.

Second, some African countries have adopted policies aimed at developing their domestic debt markets, with the active support of international financial institutions such as the African Development Bank, IMF, the Organization for Economic Cooperation and Development (OECD) and the World Bank. IMF and the World Bank have launched a joint initiative to assist countries in building bond markets by developing effective medium-term debt management strategies consistent with the goal of maintaining debt sustainability (Adelegan and Radzewicz-Bak, 2009). The African Development Bank created an African domestic bond fund in 2010 with the objective of contributing to the development of sound domestic debt markets. The fund is investable in local-currency-denominated sovereign and sovereign guaranteed subnational bonds. In 2012, the International Finance Corporation launched a bond issuance programme called the pan-African domestic medium-

Figure 9. Real GDP growth rates and depth of financial markets as measured by money and quasi money to GDP, 2000–2014

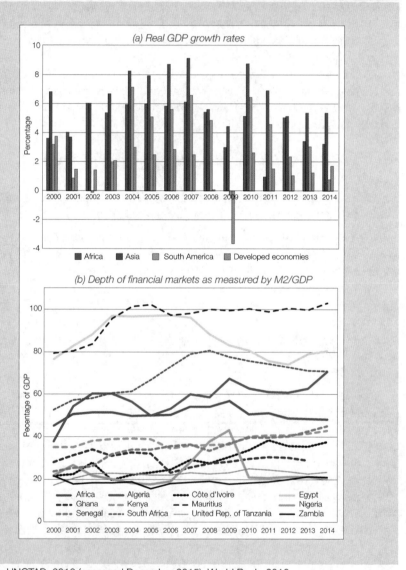

Source: UNCTAD, 2016 (accessed December 2015); World Bank, 2016c.

term note programme, initially focused on Botswana, Ghana, Kenya, Uganda, South Africa and Zambia, aimed at supporting and growing nascent capital markets in the region and increasing the availability of local currency financing for private sector development. In November 2011, the Group of 20 endorsed an action plan to support the development of local currency bond markets in emerging markets and other developing economies and called on international organizations to cooperate in data collection and analytical work on these markets, culminating in a joint diagnostic framework or toolkit designed to help country authorities analyse the state of their debt markets and identify reform priorities (IMF et al., 2013). In addition, conscious nurturing of domestic debt markets has become a major policy objective of many countries, with a number having made significant progress in broadening their investor bases, lengthening maturities and building market infrastructure.

Third, UNCTAD (2015c) shows that Africa improved in terms of financial sector development and access to banking services in 2011–2014. The depth and coverage of financial systems (as measured by the standard indicators of financial development such as ratios of broad money (money and quasi money or M2) and private sector credit to GDP have gradually improved, albeit from a low base. Nevertheless, much of this improvement is accounted for by middle-income countries, rather than low-income countries, which still have limited access to financial services. Moreover, certain groups, particularly rural populations and women, remain largely excluded from formal financial services. For example, only 20 per cent of women in Africa have access to formal financial services (UNCTAD, 2015c). Figure 9b shows the depth of financial markets in Africa as measured by the M2–GDP ratio; Egypt, Mauritius and South Africa have very deep financial markets, and these markets have supported the successful and widespread issuance of domestic debt instruments, including by the private sector. Access to banking services has also improved in recent years, with account penetration having recorded a remarkable increase of 20 per cent in 2011–2014, particularly in eastern and southern Africa (IMF, 2015a). A developed and well-functioning financial sector provides opportunities for mobilizing savings and unlocks the potential of domestic debt markets to bridge Africa's large financing gap.

Fourth, African local currency debt markets are progressively opening up to non-resident investors. While South Africa has for some time been one of the most attractive portfolio investment destinations in Africa, other markets have also managed to interest foreign investors, such as Ghana, Egypt, Morocco, Nigeria and Zambia. For example, foreign investor purchases of government securities in

Zambia re-emerged in 2004, having last taken place in 1994 (Bank of Zambia, 2015). In 2014, non-resident investors held about 20 per cent of the total outstanding domestic debt, compared with less than 0.1 per cent in 2004. Similarly, Ghana has also attracted a rising share of non-resident investors registering, in 2012, its highest net inflow, about $2.6 billion (27 per cent of total local-currency-denominated outstanding government securities). The increase in portfolio inflows in Ghana coincided with the opening of government securities markets to foreign investors in 2006 and, in Zambia, with the introduction of longer maturities for government bonds. In Nigeria, portfolio flows followed large debt relief and/or restructuring operations and renewed confidence in the country's economic prospects. In the United Republic of Tanzania, as non-residents are not allowed to hold government securities, resources from foreign investors were invested in treasury bills and bonds indirectly, with commercial banks serving as intermediaries.

The participation of non-residents in African debt markets widens the investor base. However, countries need to closely monitor the level of such participation as it may increase their vulnerability to external developments such as financial crises. Issues of previous concern that made mainstream international investors hesitate to invest in local-currency-denominated domestic debt, such as a lack of familiarity with local credits, standards and documentation, are being addressed by supranational borrowers such as the African Development Bank and the World Bank (through the International Finance Corporation).

Evolution of public debt in selected countries, 1990–2014

The structure of public debt portfolios in Africa has undergone a significant transformation since the mid-2000s. Largely due to external debt relief under the Heavily Indebted Poor Countries Initiative and Multilateral Debt Relief Initiative, total public debt ratios have declined considerably, with domestic debt becoming an important component of portfolios. This report cannot conduct a comprehensive analysis of domestic debt in all 54 African countries, but the evidence from the sample of five countries studied allows some inferences to be made of broad characteristics of domestic debt and some lessons to be learned. However, this is not a representative sample of all countries in Africa, about one third of which are classified by the World Bank as conflict-affected fragile States; given their uncertain environments, it is unlikely that they will host developing domestic capital markets in the near future.

Figure 10a shows the evolution of public debt in 1995–2013 for the sample of five countries studied. On average, external debt is much lower than in the past, having decreased from over 120 per cent of GDP in 1995 to 25 per cent in 2009, before rising to 27 per cent in 2013. The decline in external debt largely reflects debt forgiveness under the Heavily Indebted Poor Countries Initiative and Multilateral Debt Relief Initiative. These Initiatives have benefited three of the countries studied, namely Ghana, the United Republic of Tanzania and Zambia.

Domestic debt is not a recent phenomenon, as several African countries relied on this source in the 1980s, which accounted for about 11 per cent of GDP (Christensen, 2004). However, there was no discernible growth in domestic debt in the 1990s to the mid-2000s, as borrowing from the domestic market was constrained by concerns that it would induce inflationary pressures, compromise debt sustainability and crowd out private sector investments. Domestic debt considerations were significant in poverty reduction and growth facility programmes implemented in the period, with most programmes limiting the domestic financing of Governments (IMF, 2007). In Mozambique, the United Republic of Tanzania and Zambia, concerns regarding crowding out motivated limitations on domestic borrowing, while in Ghana the level and sustainability of domestic debt was the main concern behind the programme's constraint on domestic financing. Countries that ran fiscal deficits not fully matched by donor inflows would not ordinarily issue domestic debt because the standard policy advice of IMF and the World Bank was to limit domestic borrowing. In addition, poverty reduction and growth facility programmes typically included anticipated increases in aid to retire domestic debt (IMF, 2005; IMF, 2007). A common presumption was that external assistance, both concessional loans and grants, would continue to play a key role in financing poverty reduction and growth-enhancing programmes in the foreseeable future. However, these sources have proved volatile, procyclical and insufficient, given the scale of financing requirements in the region.

While countries have moved to replace declining aid flows by accessing non-concessional resources and seeking bilateral financing from emerging lenders such as the BRICS countries, recent data shows a steady rise in the ratio of domestic debt to GDP, implying that Governments are increasingly turning to domestic debt markets to meet net borrowing requirements. Domestic debt increased from 11 per cent of GDP in 1995 to around 19 per cent at the end of 2013 (figure 10a). However, the aggregate figures do not show the considerable variation in domestic debt ratios across countries (figure 10b). For example, both Ghana and Kenya

Figure 10. External and domestic debt developments for selected African countries

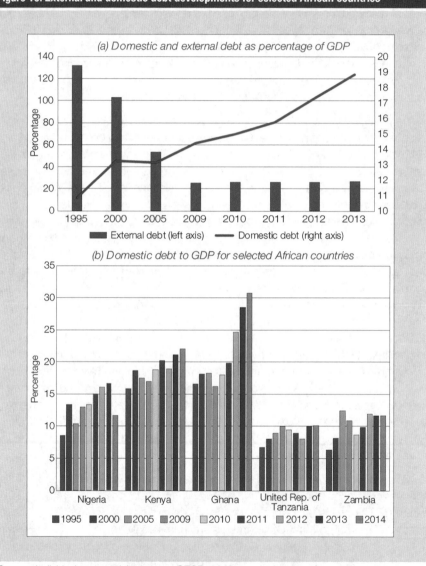

(a) Domestic and external debt as percentage of GDP

■ External debt (left axis)　　——— Domestic debt (right axis)

(b) Domestic debt to GDP for selected African countries

■ 1995　■ 2000　■ 2005　■ 2009　■ 2010　■ 2011　■ 2012　■ 2013　■ 2014

Source: Individual country debt reports; OECD, 2015a.
Note:　Data in panel (a) based on sample averages for Ghana, Kenya, Nigeria, the United
　　　　Republic of Tanzania and Zambia.

have maintained a steady increase in the ratio of domestic debt to GDP, from 17 per cent in 1995 to 31 per cent in 2014 in Ghana and from 16 per cent in 1995 to 27 per cent in 2014 in Kenya. In Nigeria, the United Republic of Tanzania and Zambia, domestic debt increased moderately as a share of GDP. While there is clearly a discernible increase in domestic debt as a share of GDP, the nominal figures are a greater cause for concern as the ratios in figure 10 are suppressed by the sustained high GDP growth in the selected countries in the last decade. In nominal terms, the increases in domestic debt are more prominent. For example, domestic debt increased in Ghana from $3.1 billion in 2005 to $10.8 billion in 2014 and in Kenya from $3.6 billion in 2005 to $13.4 billion in 2014 (figure 11).

Some countries in the region, such as Ghana, Kenya and Nigeria, have been able to meet a sizeable portion of their funding requirements through domestic capital markets. In general, domestic finance pools in African countries have been

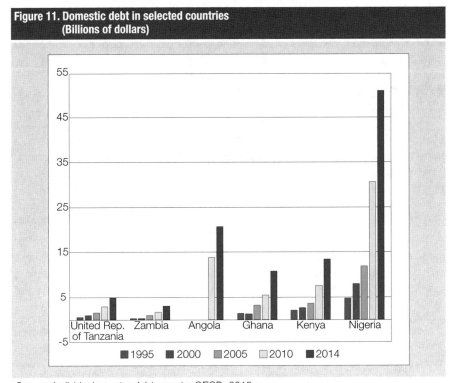

Figure 11. Domestic debt in selected countries (Billions of dollars)

Source: Individual country debt reports; OECD, 2015a.

fed by several years of high economic growth and the policy efforts of authorities, such as liberalization of capital accounts and adoption of sound macroeconomic, regulatory and prudential policies. A number of countries have also made substantial progress in developing their government bond markets, although progress has been somewhat slower in corporate bond markets.

Marketable versus non-marketable domestic debt

African Governments have increasingly met funding requirements through marketable debt rather than non-marketable debt. Marketable securities include commercial paper, bankers' acceptances, treasury bills and other money market instruments. Marketable securities are liquid, as they tend to have maturities of less than one year. Prior to 2003, marketable domestic debt constituted less than 40 per cent of the total central government debt in Kenya, Nigeria and Zambia (figure 12a). Domestic debt was held mainly by central banks and commercial banks, and was usually quasi marketable, as securities were often involuntarily acquired by these institutions in amounts that reflected the size of the fiscal deficit through reserve and liquidity requirements (figure 12b).

Domestic debt by maturity

Prior to 2001, domestic debt stocks were largely dominated by short-term instruments, usually in the form of treasury bills (figure 13a). To the extent that it existed, longer term domestic debt represented a smaller share of the total portfolio, largely held by public and quasi public institutions, including central banks. Short-term debt was predominantly in the form of 91-day treasury bills, although following high and volatile inflation in the early 1990s, authorities in a number of countries found it difficult to sell these instruments and maturities shortened even further (for example to 28 days in Zambia). A growing number of countries, many of which were previously unable to issue local-currency-denominated debt securities with long maturities, have demonstrated the ability to do so over the past decade, suggesting that the problem of original sin[24] may gradually be dissipating (figure 13b).

As shown in figure 13a, in the five countries studied, domestic debt with maturities of over 10 years averaged 24 per cent of the total outstanding domestic debt in 2014, compared with 5 per cent in 2001. In addition, all five countries issued treasury bonds with maturities of over 10 years; the largest proportion was

Figure 12.   Evolution of domestic debt in selected countries

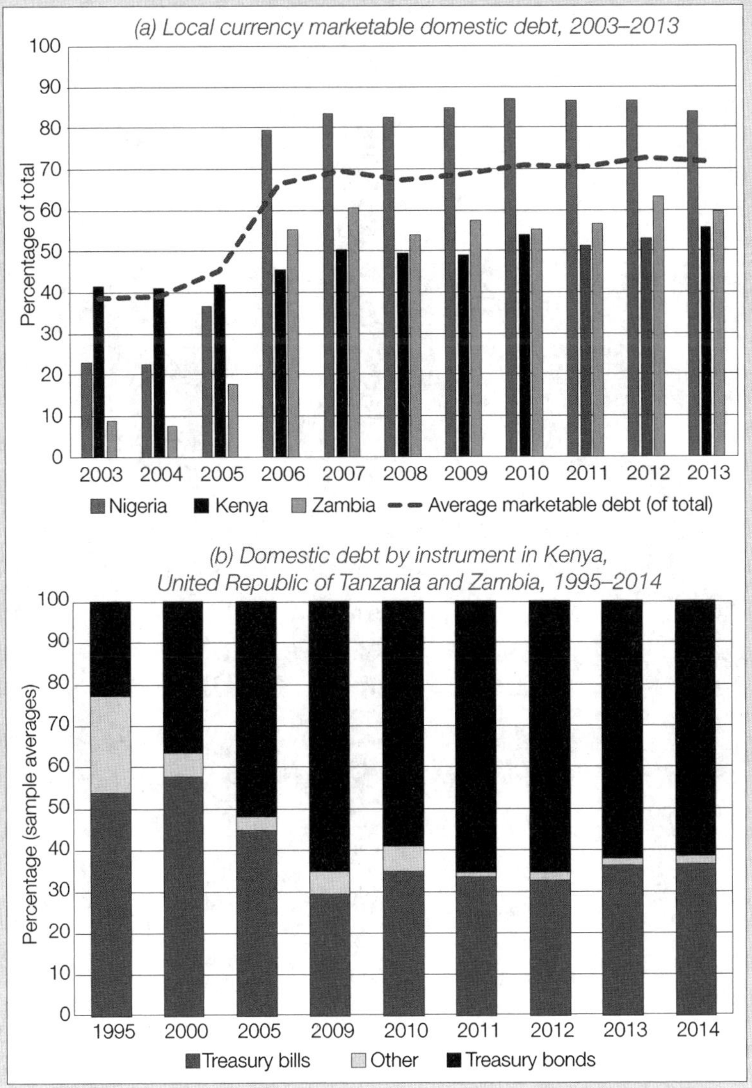

(a) Local currency marketable domestic debt, 2003–2013

■ Nigeria   ■ Kenya   ▨ Zambia   ▬ ▬ Average marketable debt (of total)

(b) Domestic debt by instrument in Kenya,
United Republic of Tanzania and Zambia, 1995–2014

■ Treasury bills   ▢ Other   ■ Treasury bonds

Source: Individual country debt and central bank reports; OECD, 2015a.
Note: Data in panel (a) based on a sample average of Kenya, Nigeria and Zambia and data in panel
           (b) based on a sample average of Kenya, the United Republic of Tanzania and Zambia.

Figure 13. Evolution in maturity of debt securities in selected African countries, 2001–2014

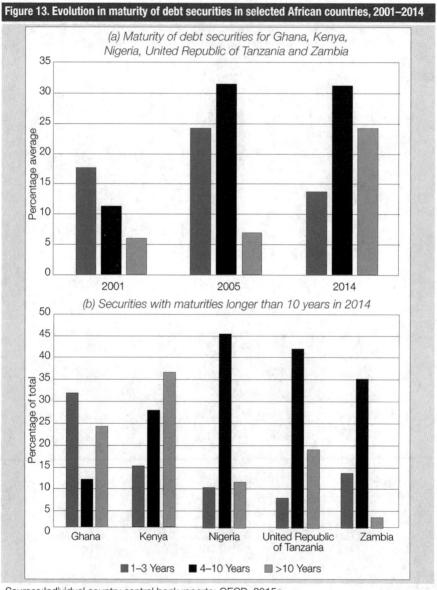

Sources: Individual country central bank reports; OECD, 2015a.
Note: Data in panel (a) based on a sample average of Ghana, Kenya, Nigeria, the United Republic of Tanzania and Zambia.

in Kenya, at 35 per cent, while Nigeria and Zambia had the smallest proportions of long-term debt, at 10 and 2 per cent, respectively (figure 13b). The shift towards long-term paper securities in African securities markets should greatly reduce rollover and market risks.

Assuming an unchanged risk appetite among international financial investors, the ability to issue long-dated instruments in most African countries is closely related to general macroeconomic conditions, in particular growth in per capita incomes, low and stable inflation rates and the emergence of large institutional investors such as pension funds. As economies grow, the demand for more sophisticated economic arrangements expands, and the need for longer term savings instruments should increase (Christensen, 2004).

Domestic debt by holder

To some extent, the growth of domestic debt since 2009 reflects the broadening of the investor base beyond traditional holders, that is, central and commercial banks (figure 14a). A number of countries have gradually given up monetary financing of public deficits in favour of debt securities financing. As a result, central bank holdings of government debt have gradually declined, although the average ratio of domestic debt to GDP has risen.

Much of the broadened investor base largely reflects the growth of non-banking financial institutions. To some extent, the decline in central bank holdings of government debt may reflect legal limits that have been put in place for such holdings. Most countries have legal limits as to how much credit a central bank may give to the Government.

Recently, non-resident demand for government domestic debt has grown. In Ghana, the share of domestic debt held by non-residents has been estimated to have fluctuated at around 20 per cent of total domestic debt (IMF, 2015a). In Zambia, foreign investors held 10.6 per cent of the total stock of government domestic debt at the end of 2014, up from 5.1 per cent at the end of 2013. The growth of non-resident interest in African government debt not only reflects recent conditions in international markets but also robust growth rates in the region. Beyond the five countries studied, South Africa is one of the countries with a significant proportion of instruments issued in the domestic market held by non-residents; holdings by non-residents rose from 12.8 per cent in 2008 to 37.2 per cent in 2014 (figure 14b).

Figure 14. Domestic debt in Africa, by holder, 2009 and 2014 and holdings of domestic marketable government bonds in South Africa, 2008–2014

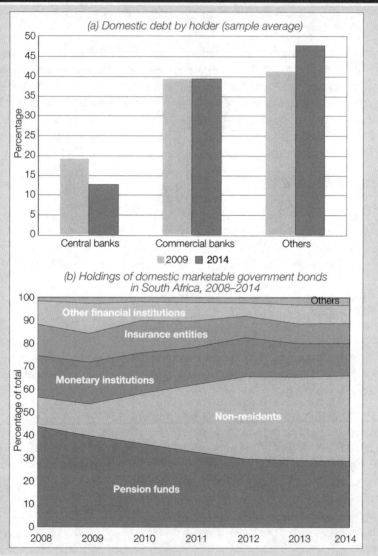

Sources: Country central banks (panel (a)) and South Africa National Treasury, 2015 (panel (b)).
Notes: Data in panel (a) based on a sample average of Ghana, Kenya, Nigeria, South Africa, the United Republic of Tanzania and Zambia. Data in panel (b) refer to holdings of domestic marketable government bonds.

The attraction of the African debt market is shown not only in the growth of foreign interest in domestic debt markets, but also in the successful sale of Eurobonds in international markets. There remains the question, however, of whether this interest will withstand a worsening economic climate.

Interest cost and burden

The main concern in relation to domestic debt is with regard to the financial cost and burden it imposes on Governments, relative to external debt. Figure 15a shows implied interest rates as proxies of borrowing costs in three countries for which data are available, namely Kenya, the United Republic of Tanzania and Zambia. On average, the countries currently face a much heavier burden on local- denominated-currency domestic debt compared with external debt. However, this is only true if the local currency is stable. If exchange rates are volatile, depreciation adds to the cost of servicing debt. For example, when Kenya issued its debut Eurobond in June 2014, the shilling was trading at about K Sh87.5 per dollar. By December 2015, the shilling had depreciated to K Sh102.3 per dollar following appreciation of the dollar in the global currency market. With this depreciation, the cost of debt service in local currency terms increased by almost 17 per cent, which had not been anticipated when the Eurobond was issued. Similarly, when Zambia issued a $1 billion Eurobond in April 2014, the kwacha was trading at about K Sh6.2 per dollar. By end-December 2015, the kwacha had depreciated to K11 per dollar, implying an additional cost for servicing the Eurobond of more than 70 per cent in local currency terms. This type of cost escalation would not occur if domestic debt instruments were issued in local currency.

However, while the nominal cost of domestic borrowing remains high, in 2000–2014, the cost of external debt showed a rising trend, particularly in 2008–2014 (figures 15a and b).[25] Many African countries are seeking to replace declining official development assistance by accessing non-concessional resources such as international capital markets, as well as bilateral financing, including from emerging lenders such as the BRICS countries, whose terms are often stricter compared with traditional borrowing sources such as the International Development Association (Greenhill and Ali, 2013; Griffiths et al., 2014). Cross-country heterogeneity leads to variations in associated financial burdens. For example, Kenya made domestic interest payments of around 2.2 per cent of GDP in 2014, while the United Republic of Tanzania and Zambia paid less than 1.5 per cent.

Figure 15. Sample averages of implied interest rates on domestic debt and interest payments on public debt for Kenya, the United Republic of Tanzania and Zambia

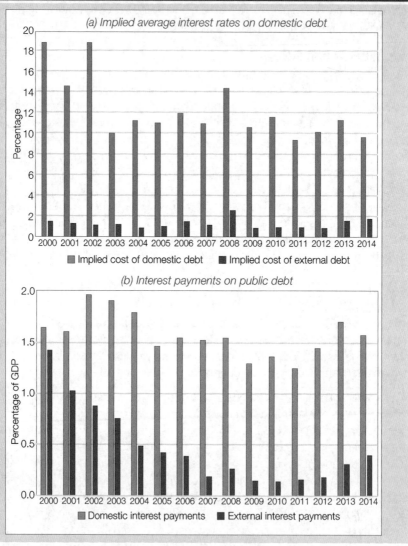

Sources: Country central banks.

Note: The nominal implied interest rate is calculated as interest payments in the current year divided by the average debt stock in that year.

C. COUNTRY CASE STUDIES ON DYNAMICS OF DOMESTIC DEBT

This section presents case studies on the dynamics and determinants of domestic debt in Ghana, Kenya, Nigeria, the United Republic of Tanzania and Zambia. In addition to the issue of data availability, these countries were selected as they have started issuing sovereign bonds in international capital markets and, as a result of capital account liberalization, have become increasingly open to both short and longer term foreign capital inflows to domestic bond and equity markets. As a result, they are not only increasingly integrating into international capital markets, but their domestic markets have become a significant source of development finance. Four of the five countries (Kenya, Ghana, Nigeria and Zambia) were among the top 10 countries in the 2014 African fundamental bond index, a ranking of African local bond markets by the African Development Bank and African Financial Markets Initiative in terms of macroeconomic conditions, governance, market infrastructure, issuers, issuing strategy and market access, domestic investor base and the participation of economic agents. The analysis in section C focused on the characteristics of public domestic debt in Africa, showing its increase as a share of GDP, as well as the considerable variation in domestic debt ratios that exist between countries. This section extends the analysis to consider key macroeconomic policies, domestic debt composition, the structure of debt in terms of maturity and the investor base. A key concern is how Africa may better foster the creation of domestic capital markets for financing Africa's development.

Ghana

In the 1980s and 1990s, Ghana, as did other African countries, had a greater reliance on concessional sources of finance. In 2000, external debt constituted almost 80 per cent of the total public debt portfolio (figure 16a). Nevertheless, although Ghana's domestic debt as a share of GDP (19.3 per cent in 1998) was similar to that in other African countries, a major source of concern was its interest burden, caused by high domestic interest rates. In October 1998, the Government carried out a national debt workshop with the assistance of Debt Relief International; among the recommendations was to set up a domestic debt fund to mitigate the burden of domestic debt service. The savings in domestic interest achieved by a donor-financed domestic debt fund were expected to lower the overall deficit and net domestic financing. Fiscal policy was programmed to aim for a zero flow of net domestic financing and net repayment of domestic debt of between 1.5 and 2.5 per cent of GDP in 2003 and subsequent years. Domestic debt declined in 2003–2004, mainly due to a sharp increase in debt relief under the Heavily Indebted Poor Countries Initiative and donor support, which resulted in an improved fiscal position. The monetary impact of the inflows was significant, as the Government used the improved fiscal position to repay domestic debt instead of reducing its net debt to the central bank, obliging the central bank to engage in increasingly large sterilization measures. In 2004–2005, net domestic financing of the budget increased by 1 per cent of GDP, mainly due to higher expenditures for poverty reduction and infrastructure in key areas, higher petroleum-related subsidies as a result of higher world oil prices and a wage overrun for government agencies.

Ghana's domestic debt steadily increased thereafter, against the backdrop of large and sustained budget financing needs. As shown in figure 16b, Ghana only realized a fiscal surplus in 2006, possibly due to grants received under the Heavily Indebted Poor Countries Initiative and Multilateral Debt Relief Initiative. Since then, Ghana has run fairly significant budget deficits. Furthermore, as a rapidly growing frontier market, Ghana has increasingly attracted foreign investors in the domestic debt market since 2006, when the Government opened the market to non-resident investors. External debt also increased gradually through a series of Eurobond issuances after 2007, under benign international financial conditions.

In recent years, the Government has faced large gross financing needs induced by weakening economic performance compounded by the sharp drop in oil and commodity prices and by power shortages. Growth decelerated from 7.3 per cent in 2013 to 4.2 per cent in 2014, and the fiscal and current account deficits widened significantly, leading to the sharp depreciation of the local currency, the re-emergence of inflationary pressures and rising interest rates. The 2013 budget sought to restore fiscal discipline and keep the national debt at sustainable levels. In particular, it aimed at reducing the overall fiscal deficit of 11.8 per cent of GDP in 2012 to 9.0 per cent of GDP in 2013. However, large shortfalls in targeted revenues as well as huge overruns in compensation to public sector workers and higher than expected interest payments affected the fiscal programme. Government budgetary operations in 2013 resulted in an overall deficit of 10.1 per cent of GDP, against the target of 9.0 per cent. The deficit was financed mainly from domestic borrowing, resulting in net domestic financing of 8.1 per cent of GDP, compared with the target of 6.4 per cent of GDP. The remaining gap in financing was funded by net foreign inflows of 2.6 per cent of GDP.

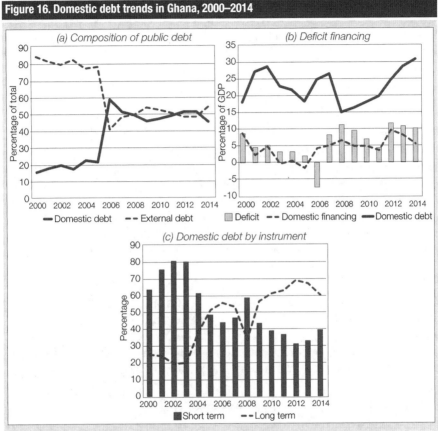

Figure 16. Domestic debt trends in Ghana, 2000–2014

Sources: Bank of Ghana, 2015; central bank debt authority reports; IMF country reports; OECD, 2015a.

In the 1990s and early 2000s, Ghana's domestic financing of the fiscal deficit was mainly done through the central bank. In the face of a large public sector borrowing requirement in 1996, the Bank of Ghana adopted an accommodating monetary policy stance by allowing deposit money banks to swap government treasury bills for its own open market operations bills. As a result, the share of government securities held by commercial banks rose from nearly 0 to about 6 per cent. In the 1990s, non-banking financial institutions played a limited role in Ghana's financial system. The largest non-banking financial institution is the Social Security and National Insurance Trust, the State pension fund.

In 2000, Ghana's debt instruments consisted of short-term treasury bills (of 91, 182 and 364 days). The only medium-term instrument available was a two-year floating rate treasury note. Long-term instruments were comprised of government stocks and revaluation stocks. Revaluation stocks had been issued in 1996 by the Government to the Bank of Ghana to remedy losses incurred in the revaluation of net foreign assets due to depreciation of the local currency. These losses had been accumulating in the books of the central bank for a long time and had resulted in negative net worth. In 2001, the Government introduced a three-year inflation indexed bond with the objective of restructuring domestic debt towards long-term instruments. In the same year, the Government took over part of the debt obligations of Tema Oil Refinery (a State-owned enterprise) to the banking system by converting them into three to five-year bonds. Other medium-term instruments, such as a two-year fixed rate treasury note, five-year government bond and a government petroleum finance bond, were introduced in 2004, and in 2005, the Government issued a Telekom Malaysia stock following the privatization of the national telecommunications company. In 2000–2004, treasury bills accounted for more than 60 per cent of domestic debt stock, and were mainly held by the banking sector. The gradual shift towards long-term instruments starting in 2005 reflects the Government's efforts to lengthen the maturity profile of its domestic debt. By 2010, at least 57 per cent of the total domestic debt portfolio was in medium- to long-term instruments and these continued to dominate thereafter (figure 16c). By the end of 2014, a large portion of Ghana's domestic debt was in long-term securities, largely held by institutional investors as well as commercial banks.

The cost of domestic debt has been increasing, following the increase in in 2014 of both 91-day and 182-day treasury bill rates by around 700 basis points to about 26 per cent. In 2006, the Government opened the domestic debt market to non-residents, but restricted them to securities with a maturity longer than three years. Holdings of domestic debt by non-residents have fluctuated at around 20 per cent of the outstanding domestic debt in recent years, presenting rollover and foreign exchange risks that may be accompanied by capital outflows and balance of payments problems.

In Ghana, there is a high level of risk that any further expansion of government borrowing in the domestic market will crowd out private sector investment and induce inflationary pressures on the economy. With regard to interest rates, Ghana maintained largely negative real rates of return on its domestic debt instruments in 2000–2009. The situation reversed in 2011, when the rates became positive. However, the non-banking sector has increasingly become a major source of financing since 2009, although the Government often relies on the central bank for funding under fiscal stress.

Kenya

In the 1980s, like many developing countries, Kenya relied on foreign concessional flows for funding development finance. However, the 1990s saw a gradual decline in development assistance to Kenya due to a failure to sustain prudent macroeconomic policies and a slower pace of structural reform (Were, 2001). As a result, the Government turned to domestic borrowing to finance fiscal deficits, resulting in the accumulation of domestic debt. In the 1990s, the Government borrowed from the domestic debt market to redeem maturing external loans. Figure 17a shows that, in the 1990s, domestic borrowing was actually higher than the fiscal deficits realized in some years in the 1990s. Other factors contributing to the accumulation of high stocks of domestic debt included stagnating real revenue receipts and heavy expenditure pressures (Maana, 2008). The annual debt management report, in June 2007, attributed the accumulation of debt mainly to reduced access to external funding and the need for domestic borrowing to finance budgetary operations.

In 2000, real GDP contracted by 0.3 per cent in the face of a severe drought, low levels of donor support, a decline in tourism, low levels of private investment and uncertainty about the Government's policy stance. The Government's fiscal programme ran into difficulties, with the overall deficit exceeding the programme deficit by 1 per cent of GDP. Recourse to arrears accumulation and a lack of finance to unwind stalled projects brought about an escalation of new claims on pending bills on the budget.

In 2003–2009, domestic debt declined from 25.5 per cent to 18.1 per cent of GDP as a result of strong economic growth, prudent fiscal policies and lower interest rates. This performance reflected the positive effects of strong revenue collection and steps taken to tighten the management of recurrent expenditures. The downward trend was reversed in the 2009–2010 fiscal year, reflecting fiscal stimulus measures implemented to mitigate the impact of the global financial crisis. Kenya's gross domestic public debt was around 24 per cent of GDP at the end of 2014. Despite a relatively low domestic debt–GDP ratio, Kenya may be vulnerable to the possible realization of contingent liabilities associated with unfunded obligations of the National Social Security Fund, the Government's current pay-as-you-go pension scheme for civil servants and the domestic debt of State-owned enterprises.

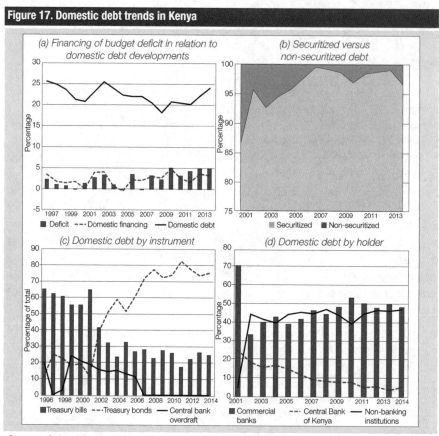

Figure 17. Domestic debt trends in Kenya

Sources: Central Bank of Kenya, 2015; central bank debt authority reports; IMF country reports;
Kenya National Treasury, 2014; OECD, 2015a.

Non-resident holdings of domestic debt are reportedly low. Domestic debt is issued mostly in the form of securitized instruments, particularly treasury bonds and treasury bills, with only a smaller proportion of domestic debt in non-securitized instruments (figure 17b). At least 80 per cent of Kenya's domestic debt has been in securitized instruments since 2001. In 2001, the domestic debt portfolio was dominated by treasury bills, at 70 per cent of total domestic debt, but the ratio consistently declined, reaching 24 per cent in 2004, and thereafter stabilized. In order to restructure the domestic debt portfolio, the Government has been issuing long-term instruments since 2001, and these constituted 75 per cent of the total portfolio at the end of fiscal year 2014 (albeit down from 82 per cent in June 2011).

Lengthening the maturity profile of domestic debt is an outcome of deliberate borrowing initiatives meant to limit the impact of refinancing risk. In the last decade, the Central Bank of Kenya embarked on a reform path aimed at developing the country's debt markets. Following the relaunch of a treasury bonds programme, and in partnership with the National Treasury and market participants, the Central Bank of Kenya initiated the creation of a Market Leaders Forum. At the time, the aim of the treasury bonds programme was to restructure the domestic debt portfolio, which had a composition ratio of 24 treasury bonds to 76 treasury bills. The objectives of the Market Leaders Forum are therefore the following: market government securities through direct linkage with potential investors; advise the Central Bank of Kenya and Treasury on various developments in debt and money markets that have a direct bearing on the performance of new issuances; and propose the floating of suitable debt instruments to diversify the product range and thereby ensure stability in financial markets. This has been the foundation for future reform measures. As a result of the Central Bank of Kenya's reform programme and the efforts of the Market Leaders Forum, the Kenyan bond market has been rated as one of the fastest growing bond markets in Africa. Some of the initiatives undertaken to lengthen the maturity profile of government-issued local debt include the implementation of a benchmark bonds programme, reopening of medium- to long-term bonds and a new debt strategy.

In 2007, the Market Leaders Forum noted that Kenya's bond market was highly fragmented, with many small bonds scattered along the yield curve. Fragmentation made the bond market illiquid, causing volatility and hampering the process of market deepening. The Central Bank of Kenya successfully started to reopen treasury bonds in 2009. Since then, the reopened issuances have recorded increased trading activity on the Nairobi Stock Exchange, which has contributed to the main objective of secondary market development. As the reopening focused on medium- to long-term bonds, the bulk of the Government's debt is now well spread between 2013 and 2041. A highly successful new instrument with long maturity, which was exempt from a withholding tax, was introduced in 2009 to finance identified priority projects in the infrastructure sector of the Government.

In 2009, the Government produced the first medium-term debt strategy, covering the 2009–2010 to 2011–2012 fiscal years. The strategy aimed to reduce refinancing risks, particularly in the domestic debt portfolio, and to further develop the domestic debt market. The Government also aimed at reducing the degree of exchange rate exposure in the portfolio. Consequently, the strategy envisaged significant reliance on domestic debt to meet financing requirements. The strategy supported the goal of lengthening the maturity of government securities and helped align domestic borrowing to the issuance of more medium- to long-term treasury bonds rather than treasury bills (figure 17c). The result was a lengthening of debt maturities, from about 4.7 years in 2009 to 6.6 years in 2012.

Commercial banks and non-banking institutions now hold roughly the same share of domestic debt, at 48.1 per cent and 46.8 per cent respectively, while the Central Bank of Kenya holds most of the remainder (figure 17d). The non-banking share increased significantly in 2002, from just under 5 per cent in 2001 to over 40 per cent in 2002, and has remained relatively stable thereafter, reflecting the greater diversification of the domestic investor base and, partly, the success of the Market Leaders Forum. The Central Bank of Kenya's holdings have declined over the years.

Kenya began to reform the retirement benefits industry by establishing a retirement benefits authority in 1997, to guide and regulate developments in the industry. This was a significant step in fostering domestic debt market development, as the Government attempted to restructure and reform the pensions sector, resulting in greater participation by pension schemes, both the National Social Security Fund and private schemes, in debt markets. In addition, pension funds were now required to invest up to 70 per cent of their assets in government securities. This requirement helped open debt markets to a new category of investors interested in medium- to long-term investment. The same strategy was adopted during the reform of the insurance industry. In January 2009, in an effort to increase participation from the retail sector, the Central Bank of Kenya reduced the minimum amounts required to invest in treasury bills and bonds from K Sh1 million to K Sh100,000 and K Sh50,000, respectively. The purpose of this initiative was to encourage retail investors to increase their savings levels by providing wider investment options and to promote financial inclusion. The current diversified investor base includes commercial banks, pension funds, insurance companies, State-owned enterprises and retail investors. Initiatives to deepen the investor base include financial literacy programmes and a proposed treasury mobile direct platform to enable easier access to government securities by the retail market.

Domestic interest payments still place a substantial burden on the economy. Since 2005, implied domestic real interest rates have been volatile. Domestic interest payments account for over 80 per cent on average of total interest payments, partly due to the large stock of domestic debt relative to external debt in Kenya. In recent years, the implied external debt interest rate has shown an increasing trend, reflecting the issuance of non-concessional debt in international capital markets. In Kenya, non-banking domestic investors have grown since 2000, providing an average of 45 per cent of the Government's funding requirements. The pension sector has grown impressively following the liberalization of the sector in 2003 and, together with reforms in the insurance sector, created demand for long-term bonds. Since 2000, credit growth to the private sector has also remained robust and banks have shown an increased willingness to place more of their excess liquid assets in government securities. Since 2008, both treasury bill and treasury bond issuances have been oversubscribed and the rate of oversubscription has been increasing. The interest of commercial banks in long-term government securities peaked in 2012 (with oversubscription in excess of 200 per cent) as yields increased due to rising inflation. The uncertainty surrounding inflation and monetary policy made government securities a preferred choice compared with lending to the private sector. Nevertheless, Kenya is one of the countries in Africa that have succeeded in developing their domestic debt markets, including the corporate bond market.

Nigeria

The ratio of domestic debt to GDP in Nigeria has been rising since the early 1980s, driven by the need to finance large fiscal deficits. In the face of decreasing foreign aid, including loans and grants, the Government has largely relied on the domestic market to fund its borrowing requirements for development finance. The portion of the deficit in the annual budgets funded domestically grew from $209 million in 2005 to $5.4 billion in 2014. As shown in figure 18a, the budget deficits have mainly been financed by domestic borrowing since 2004. Growth in the budget deficit was recently triggered by a decline in the price of oil, a major source of revenue for Nigeria. In addition to funding for appropriated budget deficits, proceeds from domestic borrowing were also utilized to fund special government stimulus-spending initiatives between 2008 and 2014. This, together with the need to fund its infrastructure deficit, contributed to the growth of domestic debt (figure 18b).

As the de facto underwriter and administrator in the primary auctions, the Central Bank of Nigeria has been the Government's main source of funding and the largest holder of government securities. There were no legal restrictions on how many government securities the Bank could purchase in the primary market, except that it was not allowed to purchase securities with maturities beyond 25 years. The Bank generally purchased most of the issues at about 5 per cent – below the market-clearing rate – keeping the Government's domestic borrowing costs artificially low.

Holding of domestic debt by the Bank has eased over the years and reached 0.2 per cent of GDP at the end of 2014 as non-banking financial entities (insurance companies, public and private pension funds) became more prominent investors in government debt (figure 18c). From 1981 to 2003, Nigeria's domestic debt was heavily concentrated in maturities of less than one year, most of which were 91-day treasury bills. Treasury bonds and development stocks had been issued for specific funding purposes in the past and, although marketable, were largely held by the Bank. This exposed the Government to high rollover and interest rate risks. These fiscal risks were further accentuated by a shallow financial system, reflected in the ratio of low money and quasi money (M2) to GDP (26 per cent at the end of 2003) and a narrow investor base. The shallow financial market unfavourably influenced interest rates and risked crowding out private sector credit in the face of the Government's large borrowing requirements. It also complicated the Bank's conduct of monetary policy, as more forceful use of liquidity management to pursue price stability could have adversely affected the Government's debt service costs.

The structural changes to Nigeria's domestic debt began in 2003, following the adoption by the Government of public debt management reforms. Apart from addressing the institutional weaknesses in the management of public debt, the reforms sought to improve domestic debt management.

First, as part of these reforms, the Government brought back a sovereign bond issuance programme that had been discontinued in 1986. This resulted in the issuance of long-dated instruments of 3, 5, 7 and 10 years, structured as both fixed-rate instruments (3-year and 5-year bonds) and floating rate notes (7 and 10 years). This was a reflection of a debt-management strategy aimed at restructuring the country's debt portfolio to achieve the 75:25 ratio of long- to short-term domestic debt. Before this programme went into effect, government borrowing from the domestic market was mainly through 91-day treasury bills; this meant that short-term instruments were inappropriately used to fund economic and social projects, which were essentially long-term assets.

Although the overall take-up fell short of expectations owing to a perceived default risk, market sentiments significantly changed following external debt relief in 2006, which enhanced the country's creditworthiness and increased portfolio flows

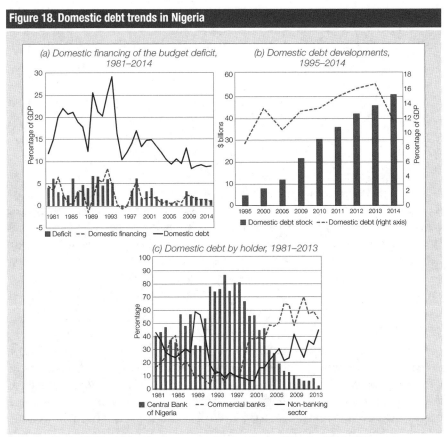

Figure 18. Domestic debt trends in Nigeria

(a) Domestic financing of the budget deficit, 1981–2014

(b) Domestic debt developments, 1995–2014

■ Deficit -- Domestic financing —— Domestic debt

■ Domestic debt stock ---Domestic debt (right axis)

(c) Domestic debt by holder, 1981–2013

■ Central Bank of Nigeria -- Commercial banks —— Non-banking sector

Sources: Central bank debt authority reports; Central Bank of Nigeria, 2015; IMF country reports; OECD, 2015a.

and foreign direct investment. In addition, its overall real GDP growth rate averaged 6.8 per cent per year between 2004 and 2014, putting it among the fastest growing emerging market economies during the period. Inflation remained stable and largely below 20 per cent. As a result, investors began to develop an interest in long-dated instruments, with tenders oversubscribed by between 60 per cent and 150 per cent between 2006 and 2014. Whereas 91-day treasury bills accounted for 62 per cent of the total domestic debt portfolio in 2003, this had fallen to 36 per cent by the end of 2014. Another major factor underlying the successful issuance of long-tenure bonds – now up to 20 years – relates to the introduction and progression of the secondary markets for government bonds, which have continued to grow. The effective functioning of the secondary market allowed investors to conveniently unwind their position in long-dated securities whenever the need for liquidity arose.

Second, a transformation in the holding structure of domestic debt took place. The Central Bank of Nigeria held about 46 per cent of the outstanding domestic debt in 2003, down from 87 per cent in 1995, while the non-banking sector held only 16 per cent, up from 9 per cent in 1995. By 2014, the Bank's holding had declined to a mere 2 per cent, while the holding of the non-banking sector rose to 45 per cent (figure 18c). The commercial banking sector's holding has also been rising at the same rate as non-banking sector participation.

This shift has important implications for the Nigerian economy: first, monetary financing of the fiscal deficit is controlled, and the Bank is insulated from a possible conflict of interests, doubling as both a fiscal agent and monetary authority; second, the investor base for domestic debt is diversified. Previous studies (Christensen, 2004) highlight the benefits of a diverse investor base in terms of lowering borrowing costs and reducing market yield volatility and potential crowding-out effects. Since 2010, Nigeria has experienced rising funding costs on its domestic liabilities. At the same time, external costs have risen, owing to the issuance of Eurobonds on market terms.

Nigeria has also attracted non-resident investors in government securities. The increased participation of non-resident investors is attributable to renewed interest in emerging markets by foreign investors because of the attractive yields. In addition, the inclusion of the Government in the globally traded J.P. Morgan government bond index emerging markets series in 2012 represented independent external recognition that the Nigerian domestic debt market had been transformed, leading to foreign participation in domestic debt instruments. J.P. Morgan subsequently excluded Nigeria from its local-currency emerging-market bond indexes after restrictions on foreign-exchange transactions had prompted investor concerns about a shortage of liquidity; nonetheless, foreign investors now have a much better perception of Nigeria's investment environment, compared with that of a decade ago.

The case study shows that Nigeria's domestic debt markets can be a major source of development finance and that the issuance of long-term domestic debt instruments is becoming less of a hurdle. Also, the investor base is widening beyond the commercial banking sector, implying a lower likelihood of crowding out private sector investment. Nigeria may not be vulnerable to external interest rate shocks, despite a high share of private creditors because of low external debt, but it would be vulnerable to a persistent decline in oil prices. This could also affect the sustainability of its domestic debt.

United Republic of Tanzania

The national borrowing strategy of the United Republic of Tanzania outlined in its 2002 budget guidelines initially focused on funding net budgetary deficits entirely from external sources, particularly concessional loans (United Republic of Tanzania, 2002). In line with this strategy, the Government sought to limit net domestic financing to 1 per cent of GDP, while maximizing concessional sources of external borrowing (figure 19a). This primary recourse to external financing had its origins in the lack of suitable opportunities for domestic borrowing, as the low level of financial market development meant that the Government could do so at a reasonable cost. In 2014, the largest proportion of the country's public debt was still concessional, but borrowing on non-concessional terms has increased in recent years.

Public domestic debt in the United Republic of Tanzania can be broken down into three components: marketable securities, non-marketable securities and other debt. Marketable securities consist of treasury bills (35, 91, 182 and 364 days) and treasury bonds (2, 5, 7 and 10 years), whereas non-marketable securities comprise special bonds and stocks. Other debt consists of non-securitized debt composed of liabilities arising from guarantees issued to government ministries, departments and agencies, and guarantees issued to public corporations, suppliers' arrears and liabilities arising from contractual and non-contractual government obligations.

Prior to 2004, domestic sources played a negligible role in funding government budget deficits, and there was no direct relationship between the increase in domestic debt and the financing of the budget deficit from domestic sources (figure 19b). Much of the domestic debt that had accumulated in the 1990s largely reflected government recapitalizations of negative net worth of State-owned banks and parastatals through the issuance of special bonds (United Republic of Tanzania, 2002). Domestic debt in the United Republic of Tanzania, at $918.2 million at the end of 2000, was one of the lowest among African countries and was not only consistent with the national debt strategy of keeping domestic borrowing low but also reflected a low national savings rate, and relatively underdeveloped debt and capital markets.

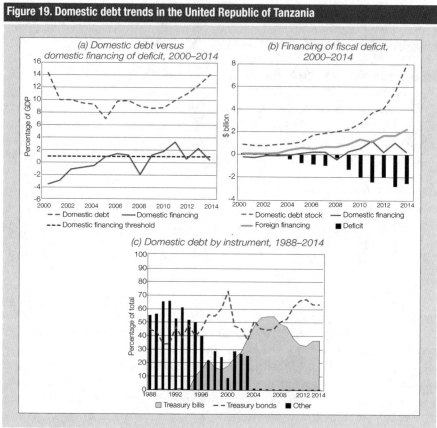

Figure 19. Domestic debt trends in the United Republic of Tanzania

Sources: Bank of the United Republic of Tanzania, 2015; central bank debt authority reports;
IMF country reports; OECD, 2015a.

However, the domestic debt stock and its ratio to GDP rose steadily between 2004 and 2014 to reach about $4.9 billion, or 14 per cent of GDP. The increase was primarily a result of growing financing needs brought about by lower government revenues, coupled with high infrastructure expenditure and the inclusion of government contingent liabilities in the debt stock. While short-term debt has remained more or less the same in recent years, a reflection of the Government's policy of the rolling over of treasury bills, there was a sharp rise in medium- and long-term domestic debt, particularly in fiscal year 2009–2010, owing to the issuance of special bonds in response to the global financial crisis and increased off-market borrowing by ministries, departments and agencies. Actual government liabilities include liabilities arising from guarantees issued to pension funds in favour of ministries, departments and agencies for implementing various projects; liabilities arising from government employees' contributions to the Public Service Pensions Fund and the Local Authorities Pensions Fund; and liabilities from compensation claims. Over time, the Government has experienced an increased demand for the issuance of guarantees in favour of the ministries, departments and agencies that enabled those institutions to obtain credit facilities mainly from pension funds to implement projects that had not been funded within the budgetary framework.

Prior to 1991, there were virtually no money or capital markets in the United Republic of Tanzania, and the financial sector was mostly owned by the State, with a few long-term non-tradable papers held by State-owned institutions. It was only in 1993, in the midst of financial sector reforms, that the Government introduced market-based treasury bills. Treasury bills were used entirely for financing purposes until 1996, when the 91-day treasury bill was earmarked as Bank of Tanzania liquidity paper. Market-based treasury bonds were introduced in 1997 to help replace the Government's non-tradable debt. Five-year maturities were added only in 2002. Special long-term bonds were issued mostly for purposes of recapitalizing State-owned banks with large non-performing loans and unsettled liabilities. Ownership of these bonds is split between the Bank of Tanzania (24 per cent) and commercial banks (72 per cent). The bonds bear either variable coupons or relatively low fixed-rate coupons, ranging from 5 to 11 per cent. Maturities range from 2 to 20 years, and interest is paid quarterly. Stocks, identical in structure to long-term bonds, arose mostly from the securitization of advances, exchange losses and other direct or parastatal liabilities owed by the Government to the banking system, in particular the Bank of Tanzania. Maturities range from 5 to 50 years, and the Bank holds 90 per cent ownership. Coupon rates vary from very high, to zero, and interest is paid semi-annually.

An analysis of domestic debt by instrument type shows that government bonds have increasingly become more dominant than any other instrument, increasing from an average of 37 per cent in 2003 to 63 per cent in 2014 (figure 19c). This development is consistent with domestic debt strategies aiming to minimize rollover risks associated with the issuance of short-term debt by lengthening the maturity profile of Government securities. As previously noted, it is important to note the existence of special long-term bonds and stocks over the years, as well as the evolution of treasury bills and bonds. There are also liquidity papers used by the Bank to sterilize foreign inflows, mainly large aid inflows. The United Republic of Tanzania experienced relatively strong growth in the supply of liquidity paper in 2005, accompanied by a sharp increase of over 2 per cent of GDP in financing paper issuance in the second half of 2005, owing to drought- and election-related spending.

In 2000, only 28 per cent of government securities were marketable. Non-tradable securities dominated, although their share has steadily decreased over time, reflecting a growing preference of both authorities and investors for market-based instruments. By 2014, at least 90 per cent of the instruments were marketable. The United Republic of Tanzania largely kept the real rates of return on its treasury securities positive. Treasury bill rates rose from a low of 3 per cent in late 2002 to an average of 15 per cent at the end of 2005 and became extremely volatile thereafter, with peaks and troughs in successive months almost 10 percentage points apart. Domestic debt issuance increased markedly between 2001 and 2005 on account of both higher sterilization operations and budgetary financing. The short duration of government securities permitted a quick and unfavourable repricing of debt. On the demand side, the rapid increase in private sector lending since 2003 has reduced commercial bank funds traditionally available for investment in government securities. While the aforementioned factors are likely to have contributed to the observed increase in yields in the United Republic of Tanzania, the highly concentrated holdings of government securities and the volatility of yields throughout 2006 and 2007 suggest that factors such as market power, strategic bidding and auction microstructure may also have been at play.

There is greater scope for domestic debt to expand in the United Republic of Tanzania without crowding out bank lending to private sector investment and inducing inflationary pressures on the economy. Given an average domestic debt ratio of bank deposits of less than 30 per cent and significant scope for financial deepening, and institutional and foreign participation in the country's financial markets, the outlook for domestic debt issuance capacity appears favourable. However, external public debt as a share of both GNI and exports is rising rapidly (table 2).

Nonetheless, a higher level of domestic debt in the United Republic of Tanzania is likely to be sustained without compromising growth, as domestic debt is issued in the form of marketable securities, bears positive real interest rates and is increasingly being issued to investors outside the banking system, particularly the pension and insurance sector. The United Republic of Tanzania has largely maintained positive real rates of return on its treasury securities since 2002.

Zambia

In the late 1960s, expansion of the government sector and high social spending were financed by revenues from the copper sector, which had undergone a boom during that decade. However, despite a range of reforms carried out through a series of structural adjustment programmes supported by IMF and the World Bank, but abandoned in the late 1980s, Zambia had a stagnating economy, a high budget deficit and accelerating inflation (Hill and MacPherson, 2004).

With the adoption of the IMF-supported Economic Reform Programme in the 1990s, the Government of Zambia managed to curb its expenditure drastically. A cash budget framework was introduced in 1993 to curtail deficit financing, based on a rule that there would be no net monetary financing of government deficits. Overall, IMF-supported stabilization programmes under the Poverty Reduction and Growth Facility sought to progressively limit domestic borrowing. This was meant to strengthen the domestic debt position and limit the crowding out of credit to the private sector. Hence, priority was placed on maximizing concessional sources of financing, with the residual deficit funded on commercial terms in the domestic market. However, domestic borrowing grew more than anticipated when concessional borrowing proved insufficient to finance the budget deficit. Significant fiscal adjustments in 2004 significantly reduced the Government's domestic financing needs, eased pressures to monetize debt and curbed crowding out of bank credit to the private sector. Since benefiting from debt relief under the Heavily Indebted Poor Countries Initiative and the Multilateral Debt Relief Initiative in 2006, Zambia has achieved higher growth and macroeconomic stability. Real GDP growth averaged 4.5 per cent per year, a marked turnaround after more than two decades of economic stagnation and falling per capita income.

In the period 2011–2014, however, large fiscal deficits were brought about by lower copper prices and sharp increases in civil service salaries. There has also been a large build-up of value added tax refund claims of exporters and expenditure arrears. IMF estimates that outstanding claims grew from 1 per cent of GDP at the end of 2013 to 3 per cent of GDP at the end of 2014. On the expenditure side, the Government accumulated domestic arrears amounting to 2.5 per cent of GDP in 2014, including to the public pension system, contractors for road projects and obligations associated with agricultural subsidies.

The correlation between domestic financing and the size of the budget deficit became stronger after 1993, following the financial reforms that resulted in the liberalization of interest rates and the introduction of a number of instruments for deficit financing. This is when the Government began to consistently fund its deficits from the domestic market. Net domestic funding grew, notwithstanding government commitments that had been elaborated in various IMF-supported stabilization programmes to limit domestic borrowing to 0.5 per cent of GDP in the medium to long term in order to avoid any crowding out of credit to the private sector. As a result, domestic debt grew quickly in nominal terms (figure 20a). In 2001, the restructuring of the balance sheets of the Bank of Zambia and the State-owned Zambia National Commercial Bank led to a large issuance of special government securities in favour of the Bank of Zambia (K1,647 billion or 12.6 per cent of GDP in 2001) and the Zambia National Commercial Bank (K248 billion or 1.5 per cent of GDP in 2002).

Loans, advances and bridge loans were government debt instruments in the form of stocks held by the Bank of Zambia. The kwacha bridge loans were funds given to the Government by the Bank of Zambia for deficit financing, while the foreign exchange bridge loans were given to the Government to finance foreign debt service shortfalls. The banking system has remained the main source of finance for the Government of Zambia, although the non-banking sector is increasingly emerging as a major source of demand. The holding of government securities by the Bank of Zambia has largely remained below 10 per cent (figure 20c), with periods of significant holdings recorded post-completion point in 2006 (19 per cent) and 2007 (15 per cent). Treasury bills have remained the main funding instrument for the Government, accounting for at least 90 per cent of the total debt portfolio between 1995 and 2000 but gradually declining with efforts to lengthen the maturity profile since 2001 (IMF, 2015b).

To foster the development of a long-term bond market, the Government introduced three- and five-year bonds in August 2005, while at the same time phasing out 12- and 18-month bonds. The introduction of long-term Government bonds reflected progress made towards improving macroeconomic stability and the Zambian financial system. It was hoped that the introduction of these securities would deliver much needed additional investment channels for institutional and other investors and provide a benchmark for the pricing of private long-term instruments. In 2005, the issuance of government securities was premised on the Government's financing requirements and the need to contain excess liquidity in

Figure 20. Domestic debt trends in Zambia

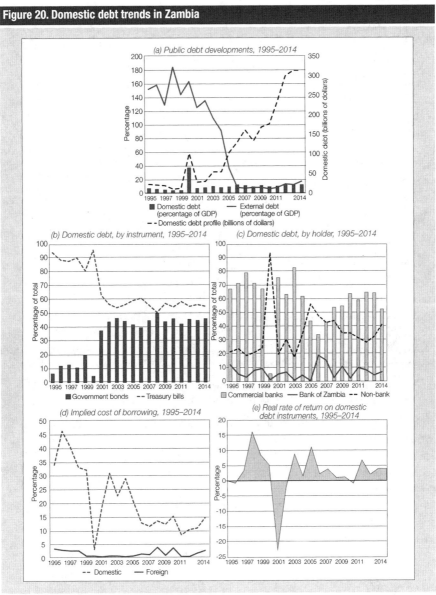

Sources: Bank of Zambia, 2015; central bank debt authority reports; IMF country reports; OECD, 2015a.

order to help reduce inflation. In this regard, the size of the weekly average treasury bills and Government bond auctions increased sharply. By the end of 2014, the share of treasury bills in the total securitized domestic debt portfolio was 54 per cent, compared with 46 per cent for treasury bonds, implying that government exposure to rollover was still high (figure 20b).

The cost of borrowing in the domestic debt market has generally been high, compared with external debt, largely an outcome of underdeveloped financial markets. The implied cost of domestic debt rose from about 34 per cent at the end of 1995 to over 46 per cent at the end of 1996 (figure 20d). However, the reduction in government borrowing between 1996 and 2000 helped lower market interest rates, with the implied cost on domestic debt falling to 8 per cent in 2011. However, recent large government financing needs have raised domestic interest rates substantially, with the one-year treasury bill rate increasing from about 12 per cent in 2012 to over 20 per cent in 2014. Consequently, the implied cost of domestic debt has risen since 2012. The annual rate of inflation rose from 7.1 per cent in 2013 to 7.9 per cent in 2014, reflecting the impact of a large increase in civil service salaries in late 2013, exchange rate depreciation in the first half of 2014 and increases in fuel prices and electricity tariffs. Despite fluctuations in its inflation and exchange rates, Zambia is one of the few countries in Africa that has managed to maintain real rates of return on government securities that are largely positive (figure 20e). This has also caused a shift in banks' portfolios from foreign assets to take advantage of the more favourable yields on domestic securities. As a result, demand for government securities has remained strong since 2006, and tenders have largely been oversubscribed.

Following the improved macroeconomic environment and confidence in the economy, foreign investor participation in government securities re-emerged in 2004, having last occurred in 1994. By the end of 2005, the stock of Government securities held by foreign investors had increased to $139.8 million (K477.5 billion) from less than $0.214 million (K1.0 billion) at the end of 2004 (table 6). As a proportion of outstanding securitized domestic debt, foreign investors held about 13 per cent at the end of 2005. Of this amount, $103.1 million (K352.2 billion) was held in treasury bills, the remainder in Government bonds. Within the treasury bill portfolio, investors held the larger portion in the 364-day maturity term, which accounted for 60 per cent of the portfolio. In the case of Government bonds, investors allocated about 47 per cent in five-year bonds. There are several other reasons for the surge in private capital flows in Zambia, particularly from hedge funds: improved macroeconomic fundamentals and more stable public policy, which reduced the country's risk premium; the lack of external capital controls; and the transparency of auctions of government securities by the Bank of Zambia.

Since 2006, the market for Zambian Government paper has become more competitive. Spreads against other emerging markets in Africa tightened substantially, with local investors, especially pension funds, seeking longer term investments to match their liabilities, often outbidding foreign investors in some auctions. The Bank of Zambia started building a system of primary dealers to encourage secondary trading in government securities.

Continued positive macroeconomic fundamentals in the economy and the relatively high yields were instrumental in attracting foreign portfolio investors in 2006–2007. However, the global financial crisis of 2008 resulted in a massive withdrawal of foreign investors from the domestic government securities market, with their participation dipping by 19 per cent by year's end. The slow pace of recovery in global financial conditions meant that foreign investors' participation in the government securities market remained subdued in 2009, after the capital flight experienced at the height of the crisis in 2008. In 2009, there was a further

Table 6. Foreign participation in government securities (Millions of dollars)							
	Treasury bills		Treasury bonds		Total		
Year	Amount	Percentage of treasury bills outstanding	Amount	Percentage of treasury bonds outstanding	Amount	Percentage of total outstanding	Year-on-year change (percentage)
2005	103.1	17	36.7	9	139.8	13	–
2006	116.4	15	54.5	11	170.9	13	22
2007	143.3	16	83.4	12	226.7	14	33
2008	90.1	14	92.6	14	182.8	14	[19]
2009	33.3	4	87.9	12	121.2	7	[34]
2010	104.9	11	27.0	3	132.0	7	9
2011	93.8	7	44.0	4	137.7	6	4
2012	137.8	10	34.4	3	172.3	7	25
2013	174.1	10	86.4	6	260.5	8	51
2014	251.4	15	190.8	13	442.2	14	70

Source: Bank of Zambia, 2015.

reduction in the overall holdings of government securities by non-residents of 34 per cent, ending the period at $121.2 million, compared with $182.8 million held in 2008. Foreign investors' holdings accounted for 7 per cent of total outstanding securities, down from 14 per cent at the end of 2008. However, as the risks associated with the global financial crisis and economic recession receded and the domestic macroeconomic outlook strengthened, foreign investors returned to the Zambian debt market in the period 2010–2014 (table 6). It is important to note that non-resident investor participation in the Zambian debt market is more prominent in treasury bills, a reflection that such investors may be sceptical about domestic macroeconomic policy consistency. This also raises Zambia's exposure to rollover risk.

There is a risk that any further expansion of government borrowing in the domestic market by the Government may crowd out private sector investment and induce inflationary pressures on the economy. Although the level of debt is moderate, given the small size of the domestic financial market and hence limited absorptive capacity, the Government could limit recourse to domestic financing to less than 2 per cent of GDP to avoid crowding out private sector credit (IMF, 2015a). Given Zambia's increasing pace of external debt accumulation, it needs to strike an appropriate balance between the need to reduce its large fiscal deficit and that of addressing infrastructure investment needs. The risk is exacerbated because a large portion of the domestic debt stock is acquired through the sale of short-term instruments. However, the non-banking sector is increasingly becoming a major source of government financing, a situation that can reduce the crowding-out effect on the private sector. The situation could be further improved by enhancing the debt management capacity of the Zambian debt office and ensuring that current government subsidies, which accounted for 2 per cent of GDP in 2014, are reduced. Pension reforms could also be accelerated to ensure the sustainability of their operations. The Public Service Pensions Fund had arrears of 1.6 per cent of GDP at the end of 2014, which the Government intends to clear by 2018 (IMF, 2015a). Borrowing from private lenders also exposes African countries to litigation by vulture funds and investment arbitration. Zambia, for example, has been prey to costly legal action by vulture funds in recent years (Pulitzer Centre on Crisis Reporting, 2014).[26]

Main findings and policy recommendations

This chapter presents new evidence of the changing patterns of domestic debt in five African countries between 1995 and 2014. First, the stylized facts emerging from the data analysis reveal the gradual increase in domestic debt, from an average of 11 per cent of GDP in 1995 to 17 per cent of GDP in 2014. Second, consistent with the results of earlier studies (Christensen, 2004), the interest burden of domestic debt is still higher than that of external debt, but there is evidence that this is declining over time, in line with deepening domestic debt markets. However, external debt has foreign exchange risks that domestic debt is not exposed to; therefore, the interest cost on local-currency-denominated domestic debt should not be viewed as a hindrance to the use of domestic debt markets to raise resources for financing development. Third, a growing number of countries have achieved the capacity to issue local-currency-denominated debt securities of long maturities over the past decade, suggesting that the problem of original sin could be gradually dissipating. In general, market depth has increased, maturities have lengthened and the investor base has broadened, making domestic borrowing much easier for Governments. Moreover, the global financial cycle may also have facilitated this process, as international financial investors have been particularly active in seeking strong yields in emerging markets.

While the risk of insufficient availability of finance for the investment required to attain the Sustainable Development Goals is still significant in a number of countries, the evidence suggests that this risk has been easing with the development of new investment interest in bonds from within countries and of foreign interest in local currency bonds. Heightened interest in bonds and improved macroeconomic stability have broadened the scope for using domestic debt to finance development in Africa. For some countries approaching lower middle-income status, a higher level of domestic debt might be sustained without necessarily compromising economic growth prospects, given that these countries have moved to diversify their investor base, made efforts to deepen their financial markets and diversified the types of instruments being issued. Nevertheless, there is scope for further strengthening of the functioning of the existing domestic debt markets, including through reform of the non-banking financial sector to widen the investor base for long-dated government securities. Further strengthening of the retirement benefits industry and the insurance sector will increase the amount of long-term finance available for the domestic debt markets.

Countries should consider both traditional and new alternative sources for financing development. The rise in domestic debt as a component of domestic resource mobilization for development finance could help reduce Africa's dependence on the volatility of foreign direct investment and official development assistance, and expand Africa's policy space. This may also strengthen policy accountability and country ownership of development strategies, as a greater reliance on domestic sources of development finance can reduce external debt vulnerabilities. However, this should be weighed against the risk incurred by increased vulnerability to changes in investor sentiment.

CHAPTER 4

COMPLEMENTARY MODALITIES FOR FINANCING DEVELOPMENT IN AFRICA

A. INTRODUCTION

The previous chapters have shown that domestic and external debt are on the rise in Africa and that ensuring debt sustainability will pose a limit to further increases in debt. With dwindling traditional financing, the question arises as to how the increasing financing needs of the continent can be met. There is a wide range of complementary modalities of development finance that tap and leverage existing resources. These modalities range from public–private partnerships, sovereign wealth funds, remittances and diaspora bonds, GDP-indexed bonds and climate-related funds to the use of new special drawing rights allocations and international reserves, and policies stemming illicit financial flows.

African countries have explored and have some experience in several of these modalities. This report focuses on three key modalities for development finance. First, this chapter discusses the merits and challenges of public–private partnerships, as they have experienced a rapid rise in Africa over the last decade, especially for infrastructure financing. Second, the role of remittances and diaspora bonds is further examined, given that they are an important source of countercyclical finance for many developing countries. Moreover, since 2010, Africa has received more foreign exchange through remittances than through foreign direct investment or official development assistance. Finally, the chapter discusses illicit financial flows, given that the scale of such flows has deprived Africa of a major source of development finance.

B. PUBLIC–PRIVATE PARTNERSHIPS

Because of the scarce availability of public sector funds, leveraging existing resources with those of the private sector has been a popular modality of alternative financing in many developing countries. In this context, public–private partnerships (box 5) have started to play a more prominent role in financing development. The last decade witnessed a considerable increase in the amount of resources invested in such partnerships in developing countries (Romero, 2015). The experience in Africa is consistent with this trend, as public–private partnerships are being used increasingly as an alternative financing mode, especially to finance infrastructure.

Infrastructure is one of Africa's major development priorities. An aspiration contained in Agenda 2063 is to have a world class, integrative infrastructure that criss-crosses Africa. In order to achieve this goal, the African Union Member States have committed to a series of actions to develop transport, energy and information and communications technology infrastructure as well as a strong commitment to mobilizing African resources to finance infrastructure development. In this regard, public–private partnerships are seen as a promising vehicle to attract private investors critical for Africa's infrastructure development. Therefore, this chapter focuses on public–private partnerships in infrastructure. The following section describes public–private partnerships in Africa to provide a picture of the magnitude and distribution of resources invested in such partnerships.

Box 5. What are public–private partnerships?

There is no single internationally recognized definition of a public–private partnership. The World Bank (2016e) , for example, defines it as follows: "A long-term contractual arrangement between a public entity or authority and a private entity for providing a public asset or service in which the private party bears significant risk and management responsibility." This definition includes public–private partnerships that offer existing, as well as new, assets and services. It also encompasses partnerships where the private party is paid entirely by service users and those in which a government agency makes some or all of the payments (World Bank et al., 2014).

The long-term component and the management of risks by the private partner is what distinguishes public–private partnerships from other types of partnership between the Government and the private sector. Typically, a private company receives a revenue stream from either the government budget, through various user charges or a combination of both. In addition to budget allocation, Governments often contribute access to land, assets and credit guarantees or provide debt and/or equity finance to cover capital expenditure. There are a wide range of infrastructure public–private partnership contractual arrangements, such as design, build, finance and operate; design, build and operate; operations and maintenance; build, operate and transfer; concessions; leases; and management and performance-based contracts.

In some ways, public–private partnerships can best be defined in terms of what they are not. They are not a form of privatization, as accountability for the delivery of a public service remains with the State. Under privatization, it is transferred to the private sector, even where the State retains regulatory powers. Public–private partnerships differ from the public procurement model, as the latter refers to the one-off purchase, lease, rental or hire of a good or service by the State. In contrast, public–private partnerships are frequently larger, they utilize more complex financial instruments and are longer term arrangements. Such partnerships have emerged as an important conduit to tackle Africa's infrastructure deficit. One of the key elements for the success of such partnerships is that they are capable of striking the right balance and transfer of risk between the public and private sectors.

Characteristics of public–private partnerships for infrastructure

Beneficiaries of public–private partnerships, values, sectors and types of contracts

According to the World Bank Private Participation in Infrastructure database,[27] infrastructure public–private partnerships are on the rise in Africa, albeit from a lower base, and account for approximately 10 per cent of the aggregate value of such partnerships globally, and 594 public–private partnership projects, worth $235 billion, have reached financial closure since 1990. Africa's infrastructure public–private partnerships are relatively smaller in magnitude and numbers than other world regions, notably Latin America and the Caribbean, and East Asia and the Pacific (figure 21).

In terms of country distribution, there is a high level of variation across Africa. Of the 52 African countries[28] considered during the period 1990–2014, Nigeria tops the list with $37.9 billion of investment, followed by Morocco ($27.5 billion), South Africa ($25.6 billion), Egypt ($24.8 billion) and Algeria ($13.2 billion). In

Figure 21. Global distribution of infrastructure public–private partnerships by project count and value, 1990–2015

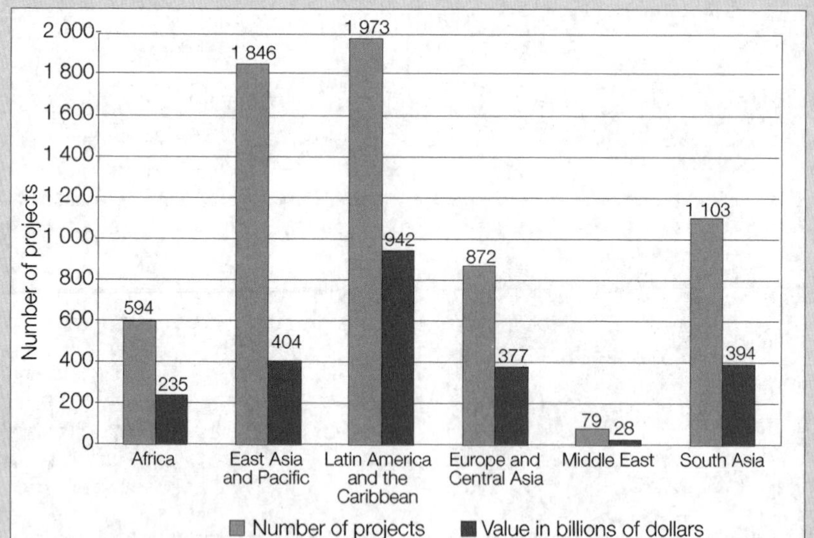

Source: World Bank, 2015b.
Note: Data refer to financially closed projects.

aggregate, these five countries account for almost two thirds of African investment in public–private partnerships. Half the continent (27 countries) has cumulative investment in such partnerships under $1 billion. Notably, the countries least exposed to infrastructure public–private partnerships in terms of value are Ethiopia, the Comoros and Swaziland, which are reported to have minimal public–private partnership investments, as illustrated in figure 22.

Figure 22. Cumulative public–private partnership investment in infrastructure, 1990–2014 (Millions of dollars)

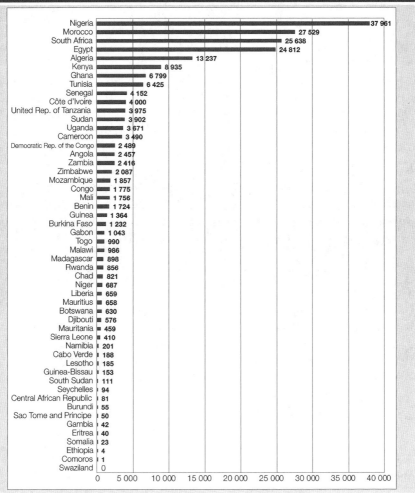

Sources: World Bank, 2015b.

Although the aggregate value of national public–private partnership investment across Africa varies considerably, the sectoral distributions of such partnerships appear to be homogenous on the whole.[29] Telecommunications rank first in most countries, accounting for 68 per cent of public–private partnership infrastructure investment. The second sector in terms of aggregate value of such partnerships is energy, which captures 21 per cent of total public–private partnership investment. The transport sector ranks third, representing 10 per cent of the aggregate value of such investment. In most countries, the sector reporting the lowest value of cumulative investment at the country level is water and sanitation, with a public–private partnership investment share of 1 per cent.

Figure 23 compares the sectoral distribution of public–private partnerships in Africa (a) and the world (b). It shows that the telecommunications and electricity sectors represent 85 per cent of public–private partnership project value in Africa, compared with 69 per cent worldwide. While public–private partnerships to build roads are ranked third on a global scale, accounting for 17 per cent of public–private partnership value, they only represent 1 per cent in Africa. Other African sectors that appear to be less prioritized are airports, water and sewerage, followed by railroads and natural gas. This is similar to the global pattern.

Public–private partnerships range from small service contracts to large-scale concessions, greenfield projects[30] and divestitures (UNCTAD, 2015c). As shown

Figure 23. Sectoral distribution of public–private partnerships in Africa and the world, 1990–2015

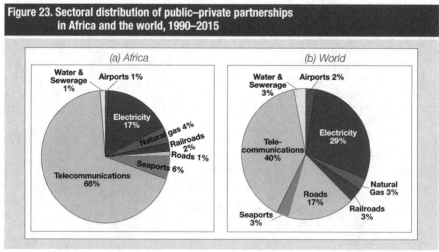

Source: World Bank, 2015b.

in figure 24, an overwhelming majority of infrastructure public–private partnership contracts – 70 per cent – are greenfield investments with an estimated value of $143.3 billion. These types of public–private partnerships are prevalent in all the four sectors described earlier, with the telecommunications sector reporting the largest value ($97.2 billion) in these types of contracts. Greenfield public–private partnerships typically envisage investments in new facilities, which may return to the public sector at the end of the concession period.

Divestiture contracts account for 22 per cent of the investment value of public–private partnerships. For the most part, such contracts are used for public–private partnerships in the telecommunications sector, and in a few cases, in the energy sector. They are relatively capital intensive, as shown by the small number of projects, representing $43.9 billion worth of investments. Divestitures imply the sale of a State-owned enterprise to the private sector. They can either be a full divestiture,[31] implying a 100 per cent transfer, or a partial divestiture, which implies that the Government only transfers a portion of the enterprise to the private sector. Morocco, Tunisia, South Africa and Egypt have the largest divestiture projects (telecommunications), which are valued at more than $1 billion.

Concession-type contracts account for 8 per cent of public–private partnership investment value, or $17.1 billion. Concessions are mainly present in energy-related

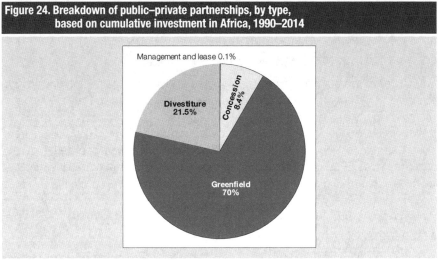

Figure 24. Breakdown of public–private partnerships, by type, based on cumulative investment in Africa, 1990–2014

Source: World Bank, 2015b.

public–private partnerships, followed by those in the transport sector. They are the more traditional types of public–private partnerships, where a private entity typically takes over the management of a State-owned enterprise for a given period, during which it undertakes significant investments and assumes related investment risks. Many African countries (27) have at least one concession contract in the transport sector and/or in the energy sector. These contracts are also intensive in terms of capital requirements; the largest one was registered by Morocco in the energy sector for $3 billion, followed by Nigeria in the transport sector for $2.4 billion.

Management and lease contracts represent less than 1 per cent of public–private partnership investment value, or $276 million. These partnerships are mainly prevalent in the water and sewerage sector, followed by the transport, telecommunications and energy sectors. Most projects operate at zero investment value, with only one project, in the Algerian transport sector, reaching $161 million. In this type of arrangement, a private entity is delegated the management of a State-owned enterprise for a given period in exchange for a fee. In management contracts, the Government remains the principal risk taker; in lease contracts, the Government delegates the risk to a private operator. In both contract modalities, the Government continues to own the enterprise and make investment decisions.

Drivers of public–private partnerships for infrastructure

Rationale for using public–private partnerships

Public–private partnerships are becoming increasingly popular, given the expected and associated benefits of such partnerships.

They have the potential to provide access to additional sources of funding and financing by leveraging existing resources with those of the private sector and improving the quality of public services. Through these partnerships, Governments could attract and access specialized skills, technologies and innovation from the private sector, leading to greater operational efficiency, hence better quality public services. Public–private partnerships may thus be attractive instruments for developing countries seeking to improve the quality and competitiveness of their services base. This is particularly true for infrastructure services, such as telecommunications, where competitiveness depends on a high level of expertise and cutting-edge technology (UNCTAD, 2015c).

However, efficiency gains need to offset the higher financing costs of public–private partnerships so as to generate additionality of resources. Financing costs of such partnerships tend to be higher, given that private partners generally face higher financing costs than the public sector. The Trade and Development Report, 2015 (UNCTAD, 2015b) thus cautions the expectation of public–private partnerships leading to the allocation of additional resources to the public sector. The Report states that on a global scale, the results in terms of additionality are at best ambiguous, as the results in terms of improved efficiency are mixed.

In the African context, however, public–private partnerships have led to an extension of new infrastructure services, which suggests additionality. Moreover, it could be argued that both private partners and Governments have shown a continued and increasing interest in public–private partnerships.[32] This may be representative of many African countries struggling to secure financing for infrastructure projects. When Governments are credit constrained so that they cannot borrow, public–private partnerships are a potential financing modality.

Other associated benefits are related to training and professional development, research and development and knowledge sharing. Public–private partnerships are a means of developing local private sector capabilities through joint ventures with large international firms, as well as subcontracting opportunities for local firms in areas such as civil and electrical works; facilities management; and security, cleaning and maintenance services (UNCTAD, 2015d).

Public–private partnerships may offer an alternative to lending on the capital market or privatization. Compared with privatization, the Government does not need to relinquish control of a public service, as it circumvents complete privatization (Qizilbash, 2011). Moreover, such partnerships allow sharing the risk of a project between the public and private sectors. When risks are allocated adequately, depending on the management of risk capabilities, the overall project cost for the Government can be reduced. Typically, the private sector would bear construction and environmental risks, while the public sector assumes regulatory and foreign exchange risks; commercial and financial risks are shared. Perhaps what most distinguishes public–private partnerships from other development finance vehicles is their flexibility. These instruments can be tailored to meet the specific needs of a contractual relationship between the public and private sectors.

Regional push for public–private partnerships

At the regional level, public–private partnerships are being used to finance large transnational projects in the telecommunications, transport, water and energy sectors in a significant number of African countries. There are several initiatives and programmes at the pan-African level that focus on public–private partnerships. Under the New Partnership for Africa's Development, public–private partnerships are considered a promising vehicle to attract private investors critical for Africa's infrastructure development (African Union, 2001).

The Programme for Infrastructure Development in Africa also recognizes the value of such partnerships. According to the Programme, many countries are unable to fully harness private sector interest in infrastructure projects for lack of enabling regulations, local skills and an adequate understanding of the risk allocation of public–private partnerships. Furthermore, this may be curbing the potential for such partnerships in Africa's transformation (African Union et al., 2010).

Regional economic communities[33] are making efforts to improve on this situation by addressing public–private partnerships through modal regulation and/ or instruments. An example of this is the Economic Community of West African States Energy Protocol, which seeks to promote the development of various energy programmes by harnessing private sector energy investments. The Protocol has also served as a basis for the agreement establishing the West African Power Pool, which includes 14 Member States of the Community and sets the framework for the engagement and association of public and private power entities comprising the Pool.

Yet another example of emerging regional policies and regulations that cater for such partnerships is the Southern African Development Community regional framework for public–private partnerships. This framework prioritizes infrastructure development in the 15 members of the Community and provides a set of principles and guidelines based on experiences in public–private partnerships to support institutions in the region that are involved in the development and management of such partnerships. Along the same lines, the Common Market for Eastern and Southern Africa (COMESA) in late 2013 issued the Monitoring and Evaluation Policy Framework for its 20 Member States, in an effort to harmonize public–private partnership structures in the region.

Another interesting initiative can be found in the East African Community: a legislative and institutional framework for public–private partnerships in the infrastructure sector. Launched in 2012, the public–private partnership Project Advisory Unit Network aims to assist the Community in building capacity in Member States to be better able to harness public–private partnerships in infrastructure services. From a policy perspective, these efforts are viewed as conducive to the development of a regional policy on public–private partnerships that will need to look at regulation, standards and policy harmonization across the Community (World Bank, 2014).

In addition, public–private partnerships are implicitly addressed in a number of regional investment protocols, such as those of COMESA, the East African Community, the Economic Community of West African States and the Southern African Development Community. For example, the Investment Agreement for the COMESA Common Investment Area establishes the COMESA Common Investment Area, with a view to promoting COMESA as an attractive investment area, among other objectives (article 2). As such the agreement defines investment (article 1.9) as "assets admitted or admissible in accordance with the relevant laws and regulations of the COMESA Member State in whose territory the investment is made" and further provides a positive list of what is considered to be investment. This list includes, among others: "business concessions conferred by law or under contract, including build, operate, own/transfer, rehabilitate, expand, restructure and/or improve infrastructure; and concessions to search for, cultivate, extract or exploit natural resources." These are traditional forms of public–private partnerships.

The same applies to rules of investment in the Economic Community of West African States. A supplementary act adopting community rules on investment and the modalities for its implementation within the Community contains an investment definition which includes "contractual rights, such as under turnkey, construction or management contracts, production or revenue-sharing contracts, concessions or other similar contracts".[34] Equally so, the Southern African Development Community Protocol on Finance and Investment defines investment as "rights conferred by law or under contract, including licences to search for, cultivate, extract or exploit natural resources".[35]

Public–private partnerships are also being covered through existing investment regulations in the regional economic communities, although the implications of this are too early to be assessed. Potentially, a public–private partnership contract covered by any of these existing agreements made by an investor of one of the Member States could have recourse to the existing dispute-settlement mechanism provided for in these various investment protocols. This in itself could lead to litigation dealt in domestic and regional courts, which in turn may have implications on the institutional capacity to better understand the regulation and contract clauses of public–private partnerships.

Challenges and risk factors of public–private partnerships for infrastructure

The experiences of many countries in public–private partnerships as a financing modality have revealed several challenges and risks, which are discussed in this section. The most important is the risk that such partnerships could become a fiscal burden, which merits a careful analysis in the context of Africa's development finance.

Public–private partnerships as a contingent liability and their impact on debt sustainability

Public–private partnerships are often treated as off-budget transactions known as contingent liabilities. This implies that obligations on the part of the Government are not immediate and are dependent on certain conditions. They can be explicit when contained in contracts or when they take the form of guarantees expressly formulated by a Government. While this mechanism or treatment provides countries with some flexibility to expand their fiscal space, it can generate liabilities.

For example, although a debt in respect of the infrastructure in public–private partnerships is officially taken on board by the private sector and does not appear on the Government's books, such partnerships give rise to obligations on the part of the Government to purchase services from a given private operator and to honour calls on guarantees (Jubilee Debt Campaign, 2012). However, because such obligations usually take time to materialize, and guarantees only become effective when public–private partnerships fail or underperform, they are often considered contingent liabilities by the Government; hence they are not usually factored into government budgets.

There are also implicit liabilities when a Government would have to assume these, even though it may not have provided a guarantee (Martin, 2015). For instance, the Government may need to become involved with private sector debt on the part of a private company with which the Government has a public–private partnership arrangement. If this debt is considerable and becomes unmanageable by the private company, this could result in the financial overheating of the domestic banking sector and lead to systemic risk, if unresolved. It could lead to a crowding out or even a shortfall of liquidity. Here, the Government would have to step in to bail out the private company that incurred the debt with private banks and might have to use existing fiscal resources to contain that risk, with implications for government commitments in other sectors.

It is therefore understandable that public–private partnerships have the potential to incur a high fiscal cost and can entail risks for debt sustainability over time. In other words, the failure of a public–private partnership can have the potential to generate a fiscal squeeze, since Governments are held liable for the obligations they incur contractually under an agreement. In capital-intensive infrastructure projects that are government guaranteed, the implications can be serious, particularly for small economies, which would then have to use existing revenues and/or incur more debt to be able to finance budgeted activities and existing commitments.

In addition, when projects are financed through international lending, they entail foreign currency exposure for both debt repayments and dividends. While returns are in local currency, an exchange rate shock affects the ability of the Government to repay and project profitability (UNCTAD, 2015b).

In the broader context of external debt management, estimates of the impact of contingent liabilities on debt sustainability are normally not included in the standardized stress tests of the current debt sustainability framework (IMF, 2013a).[36] As public–private partnerships are often treated as off-budget transactions, they may encourage countries to use them to circumvent national or IMF-agreed debt limits (Griffiths et al., 2014).

It is therefore important that a Government fully understand the type of contractual arrangement it undertakes and that it assess the risks for debt sustainability. Caliari (2014) and Prizzon and Mustapha (2014) show that public–private partnerships might have implications for debt sustainability, which consequently may pose a challenge for development finance.

Given the potential impact of these instruments on public debt, it is necessary to consider how to address the liabilities through effective debt management. An improved monitoring framework in terms of macroeconomic risk that adequately quantifies contingent liabilities in the form of public–private partnerships is especially desirable for infrastructure financing, which is capital intensive and where associated risks are seldom known in advance.

Other challenges and risk factors

Public–private partnerships are complex undertakings, especially those related to infrastructure. They involve several partners related to each other through complex contractual arrangements and different incentives; they tend to have long-term time horizons and are generally capital-intensive projects. These factors represent considerable risk.

Public–private partnerships face challenges stemming from a lack of or inadequate regulation. This leads to uncertainty and works as a disincentive for investment, as contracting partners cannot resort to a legal system that predictably protects their investments in case of conflict. Furthermore, there are information asymmetries such as insufficient data on the creditworthiness of the partners of a public–private partnership. As a result, the cost of the partnership could increase, as the Government needs to provide guarantees to cover the implied risk.

Other modalities to cater for regulatory challenges pertain to the inclusion of contractual clauses containing dispute-settlement mechanisms that seek legal redress in internationally recognized venues for commercial or investment-related disputes. However, these instruments may generate additional challenges and costs to the parties involved in public–private partnerships – especially Governments – when involved in an investment dispute.

There is also a component of legal risk, or litigation risk, which is associated with differences in the interpretation or violation of public–private partnership contracts in the broader context of bilateral investment treaties. Such treaties offer protection to investments, and because public–private partnerships are often considered to be a form of investment, Governments can be legally liable if the private partners are protected under a bilateral investment treaty their host country has signed with the Government in question.

There are various challenges and risks involved in the design and implementation of public–private partnerships. The main challenges include the opacity of the issuance and awarding of public–private partnership contracts; a changing incentive structure, depending on the stage of the partnership; how to ensure an optimal distribution and allocation of benefits in the short, medium and long terms; and how to meet and maintain associated quality and sustainability standards during and beyond the life cycle of a public–private partnership.

From a sustainable development perspective, force majeure and environmental risks, especially those associated with project development in various infrastructure sectors, should be considered. For example, the possibility of a long-lasting drought occurring during the life cycle of a public–private partnership that is being operationalized to build a dam to source a hydroelectric plant can have major implications on the expected returns on investment and overall performance of a public–private partnership. Environmental impact assessments are typically also part of the process of large infrastructure public–private partnerships, but these, too, cannot fully account for potential climate change-related or other natural events that may be categorized as force majeure.

Furthermore, there is a risk of power imbalance when the Government deals with a corporate entity with market power comparable to or even greater than its own. This can lead to imbalances when the terms of a contract are negotiated and can result in a situation where the partner company can be large and powerful enough to take on the regulators in case of conflict (Shaoul, 2009).

Challenges and risks are also associated with the opportunity costs of public–private partnerships. The costs associated with such partnerships are often non-transparent and non-accountable to auditors, parliaments or civil society. Public–private partnerships usually require upfront fiscal incentives and/or transfers from the host Government, which are difficult to quantify ex ante and are normally not recorded as government finance. For example, Governments may provide for a tax holiday on the acquisition of machinery to a company building a road in the context of a public–private partnership. In general, this will not be accounted for, but will represent a liability in terms of foregone revenue from the tax that was exempted and that could normally have been used to fund government expenditures in social and health programmes.

Another related cost under public–private partnerships is associated with the type of services provided by private operators. Such agreements have implicit opportunity costs in terms of foregone revenues from levying tariffs or user fees (Caliari, 2014). There is also evidence from other regions that these implicit opportunity costs may also produce mixed results in terms of the quality and performance of public–private partnerships (UNCTAD, 2015b; United Nations Economic Commission for Latin America and the Caribbean, 2011).

Reservations have also been expressed about the limitations of public–private partnerships on financing development, as these are considered to be among the most expensive financing modalities (Griffiths et al., 2014). It is estimated that such partnerships may represent three to four times the costs of bonds, and lenders to the private sector will demand 3 to 5 per cent more interest than public loans (Martin, 2015). In the context of national development, this also raises the opportunity cost in terms of what a Government could have alternatively financed if the additional costs of public–private partnerships had not been incurred. This ultimately poses a burden on debt management, as these additional costs generally imply that a Government would need to seek additional resources to cover the resulting financing gaps from diverted budget revenues to cover these costs.

As a rule, public–private partnerships include more risks than development projects exclusively financed through private sources. The reason is that many such partnerships would normally not be considered bankable in the traditional sense because of the various risks involved in the development of these financing projects. Indeed, public–private partnerships only become commercially viable because the Government traditionally guarantees the investor against the various associated risks involved in the implementation of these development projects. It is all the more critical for Governments guaranteeing public–private partnerships to have the capacity to understand the exposure they may face when engaging in such partnerships, and this is a major challenge in many countries.

How likely public–private partnerships for infrastructure are to fail

In Africa, a total of 60 public–private partnership projects in the infrastructure sector are known to have been cancelled or distressed.[37] They are valued at $1 billion and represent 4 per cent of the total value of investment (table 7). Although the percentage of the investment that has been at stake in the context of these public–private partnership failures is minimal (4 per cent), it still represent a financial burden borne partially or fully by the Government, the guarantor of these agreements in most instances.

The share of failing public–private partnership projects in Africa is relatively low, compared with South-East Asia and Latin America. Between 1990 and 2014, 89 projects were cancelled or qualified as distressed in South-East Asia, representing

Table 7. Cancelled or distressed public–private partnerships, 1990–2014

Subsector	Project count	Total investment (millions of dollars)	Percentage of total investment
Airports	3	377	0
Electricity	17	1 368	1
Railroads	5	619	0
Seaports	2	25	0
Telecommunications	30	4 372	3
Water and sewerage	3	9	0
Total	60	1 030	4

Source: World Bank, 2015b.
Note: Individual country information was not available for Algeria, Djibouti, Egypt, Morocco and Tunisia.

9 per cent of total investment in that region. In Latin America, there were 146 such projects, which accounted for 6 per cent of total investment in the region.[38] These two regions have been considerably more exposed to public–private partnerships, which may partly explain the higher incidence of risks and failure of such partnerships. Arguably, Africa could also have benefited from the experience of other regions to better manage public–private partnerships and thus prevent failure. Another reason could be related to risk aversion; African countries may limit their engagement in public–private partnership arrangements to projects that are considered less risky.

Mitigating risks and policy recommendations for sustainable public–private partnerships

A major question that arises in the context of this analysis is how to address and mitigate these various types of risk. More fundamentally, what needs to be in place for public–private partnerships to function well and deliver the expected benefits and returns? Also, what is the experience of African countries in dealing with public–private partnership issues at the policy level?

Setting up a public–private partnership policy framework that addresses and mitigates these risks is a major challenge. It requires a complex set of legal, managerial and technical capacities to clarify the roles and responsibilities of contracting partners, provide clarity in case of litigation, plan and monitor implementation effectively and carry out robust investment appraisals and financial analysis.

A study carried out by the New Partnership for Africa's Development (Farlam, 2005) noted that public–private partnerships have been most successful where there is thorough planning, good communications, strong commitment from all parties and effective monitoring, regulation and enforcement by Government. Governments must improve the way they deal with the aforementioned risks to realize the efficiency and effectiveness gains that public–private partnerships offer.

It is important to have an adequate contingent liabilities management framework that accompanies and supports Governments during the life cycle of a public–private partnership and allows for the early identification of risks, such as early terminations or alterations of contracts, and an adequate response in terms of corrective action to prevent failure. This calls for standardized financial reporting, which regularly evaluates the costs and risks of the direct and contingent financial obligations imposed during project implementation. Risk-based pricing is a valuable tool in assessing the explicit and implicit costs of public–private partnerships. An appropriately priced public–private partnership helps to ensure the viability of a contract and to pre-empt the possibility of failure.

Another way to improve the management of the associated risk is to monitor the implementation of public–private partnerships. For example, a public–private partnership governing board may be formalized through inter-agency committees, which monitor implementation on a regular basis. In addition, provisions may also be made for a contingent liabilities fund that is kept at the treasury or central bank to cater for the management of public–private partnerships that fail, and that may only be accessed with the board's permission.

From a debt management perspective, Governments should not be forced to turn to riskier funding because of limited financing alternatives. Indeed, most countries may not have adequate budgetary contingencies for infrastructure financing, which is why guarantees are often used to attract private investors to fund infrastructure projects. Public–private partnerships are a good source of funding when used primarily to attract a particular expertise that is not available.

Transparency and proper risk allocation are two important components of well-functioning public–private partnerships. Greater transparency can be promoted through a listing of projects and possibly also the vetting of these projects by the general public. Risk allocation can be achieved by upholding several risk management principles, notably those of identifying and allocating risk to the party best placed to manage such risk, practising adequate risk pricing and taking necessary mitigation actions to reduce the chances of risk (Kauf, 2015).

Having the expertise and competencies to understand and assess the complexity of public–private partnership contracts is essential. Handling these associated risks requires adequate screening and foresight, especially when it comes to determining the financial burden these instruments may represent for a Government.

Regulatory bodies overseeing public–private partnerships will require support and institution building in the public sector. The emerging intentions and efforts to regulate public–private partnerships in many African countries and regional economic communities should also be accompanied by sufficiently autonomous institutions that oversee the functioning of such partnerships. In the Economic Development in Africa Report 2015, it was recognized that although the State remains a major player in the provision of infrastructure services, regulatory independence is an important element of effective infrastructure services provision (UNCTAD, 2015c), and hence in supporting public–private partnerships as well.

As Governments and regional economic communities develop public–private partnership policies and instruments, they may also need to consider creating dedicated public–private partnership units to ensure transparency, tackle problems and bottlenecks in the public–private partnership process and protect the public interest. Governments may also need to fast-track legislation which reforms the procurement culture often associated with public–private partnerships, making it more transparent and outcome oriented, especially during project selection. These institutions will need to be vested with the necessary powers and independence to be fit for purpose in their supervisory roles of these types of contracts. They will also need to have adequate mechanisms in place to be able to act whenever public–private partnerships fail and ensure the highest standards of quality, accessibility and affordability for the general public and the benefit of Africans as a whole.

The role of absorptive capacities should be highlighted in this regard. As the success of a public–private partnership depends on Governments having a conducive regulatory framework, this partly explains why many developed African countries have turned to public–private partnerships.

Regional investment regimes concerning public–private partnerships may represent an opportunity to harmonize policy relating to such partnerships and deal with them in a more coordinated and coherent manner. This will be particularly relevant to public–private partnerships that span several countries within the African subregions. Importantly, investment agreements regulating public–private partnerships can generate additional risks posed by litigation. In the context of regional investment treaties, this could lead to litigation in domestic and regional courts. This may have implications in terms of institutional adjudicatory and regulatory capacity to better understand regulation and contract clauses concerning public–private partnerships in the future.

Two major challenges in this regard are the ability to learn from the pitfalls of experiences in public–private partnerships in Africa and build the capacity to adopt best practices from the African subregions. To do so, greater dissemination and sharing of what is working in public–private partnership design and development is necessary. In addition, resources should be channelled for training and capacity-building so that public sector officials at the country and regional levels can build adequate expertise in and increase their knowledge of the management of such partnerships.

Box 6 provides a snapshot of how African countries have dealt with public–private partnership policies at the national level. It reveals that while countries include such partnerships in their respective development plans, they do not specify how they can be conduits for development. Very few countries have dedicated policies or regulations in place for their own domestic use, but a number of countries have recognized this gap and have indicated the desire or intention to develop such instruments in their development plans.

Lastly, there is a new category of partnerships: pro-poor public–private partnerships. These incorporate some of the strategies and methods of the informal sector, while specifically targeting the most vulnerable sections of the population. By including local communities and civil society as key stakeholders during negotiations and establishing a funded system to monitor and assess a project's impact on the poor, these partnerships are designed to help the poor.

Box 6. National policies on public–private partnerships

Examining how public–private partnerships are treated in the context of national development plans can be revealing in terms of their policy relevance and the extent to which they have been mainstreamed into existing national development visions in African countries. The national development plans of 35 African countries[1] were reviewed in a non-exhaustive mapping exercise conducted for this report. Five main questions were asked to assess the extent to which the partnerships were viewed as a conduit for achieving a country's national development objectives. The results are indicated in figure 25.

While 29 countries establish a link between public–private partnerships and national development goals, there is considerable variation as to how countries classify public–private partnerships and how they articulate the use of such partnerships in their broader development vision. Many of the formulations in national development plans lack a certain degree of specificity. In other words, although they are viewed as conduits for development, it is not clear how they may contribute to a country's development. This could be explained by the lack of documentary evidence of the developmental impact of public–private partnerships.

When assessing development priorities from a sectoral perspective, 30 countries of the sample clearly link or target public–private partnerships to specific sectors in their national development plans. In all of these countries, public–private partnerships are viewed as a funding model for infrastructure projects by mobilizing private sector sources in an efficient way to share the risks, while alleviating the financial burden of the Government.

With regard to specific legal or policy instruments referred to in such partnerships, 18 of the 35 countries of the sample mention various legal or policy instruments. Some

Box 6 (contd.)

countries provide a relatively detailed account of policies dealing with aspects of public–private partnerships and make specific reference to existing legislation or policy. Others are forward looking, signalling the intent to regulate or develop policies for such partnerships in the near future.

When determining whether public–private partnerships are mentioned in association with regional integration or regional economic communities of which countries are members, the mapping exercise reveals that only two countries clearly relate public–private partnerships to this dimension of the analysis. The absence of linkages between such partnerships and regional integration projects and programmes across a majority of national development plans contrasts with the advancement of regional infrastructure development projects.

⁷ Algeria, Angola, Botswana, Burkina Faso, Cameroon, Cabo Verde, Chad, the Congo, Côte d'Ivoire, Djibouti, Ethiopia, Gabon, Ghana, Guinea, Kenya, Lesotho, Libya, Madagascar, Malawi, Mozambique, Namibia, the Niger, Nigeria, Rwanda, Senegal, Seychelles, Somalia, South Africa, South Sudan, Swaziland, the United Republic of Tanzania, Tunisia, Uganda, Zambia and Zimbabwe. National development plans were available for these countries.

Figure 25. Relevance of public–private partnerships in African development plans

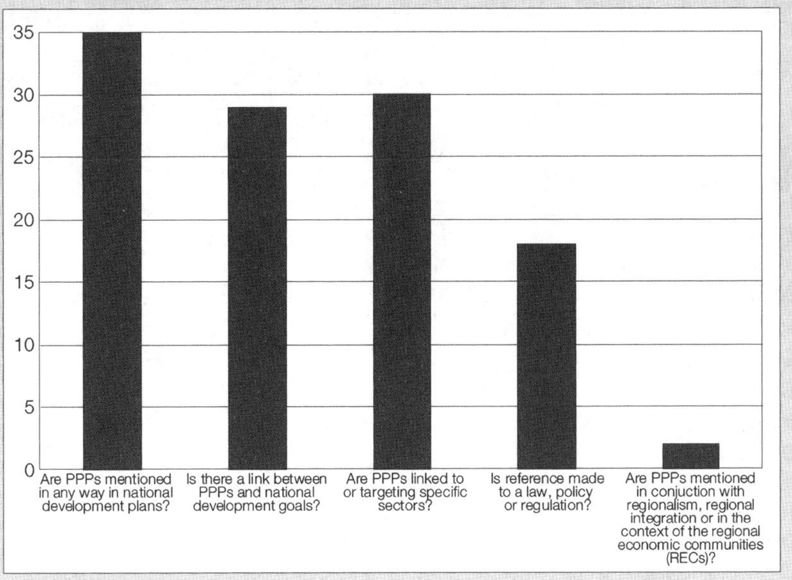

Source: UNCTAD secretariat.

Notes: Y axis indicates number of countries with a positive response to the survey question.
       Abbreviation: PPP, public–private partnership.

Conclusions

In many African countries, public–private partnerships are on the rise. From this analysis it has become apparent that such partnerships are important vehicles for financing capital-intensive infrastructure development projects, both at the national and regional levels. Despite being considered by some as the costliest types of financing sources, they are readily used across Africa and are expected to continue rising in popularity. Indeed, many public–private partnership projects and investments are under way and are financing infrastructure development projects. Virtually all African countries have experience in such partnerships. In addition, many countries have or are in the process of developing public–private partnership-related regulations and/or policies, to better harness this type of investment in these various sectors, as indicated in many national development plans.

At the regional level, African subregions are also engaging in public–private partnerships, particularly in the energy sector, as exemplified by the West and Southern African power pools. It could be argued that such partnerships are becoming an important vehicle to promote developmental regionalism. Regulation is emerging slowly, but public–private partnerships are progressively being included in regional protocols and agreements that focus on sectors such as energy, investment and public–private partnership-specific frameworks from a subregional perspective. This is an important development that could potentially boost the attractiveness and bankability of regional infrastructure projects, while promoting the harmonization of public–private partnership contracts, as well as relevant regulation.

Public–private partnerships are not the sole solution to financing infrastructure in Africa and are not a panacea; therefore, it is important for policymakers to assess on a project-by-project basis when and under what conditions such partnerships should be considered. Often the main benefits of such partnerships are the innovation, expertise and specialized management and services delivery introduced by the private sector, in addition to the investment.

Managing risk in the context of public–private partnerships is a major challenge for ensuring both debt sustainability and continuity for development. Given their nature, such partnerships are characterized as contingent liabilities, meaning that the risk of failure for these types of projects is unknown. It is therefore important to have an adequate contingent-liability-management framework that accompanies and supports the Government throughout the life cycle of a public–private partnership and allows for the early identification of risks and adequate response in terms of corrective action to prevent the failure of such partnerships, which could result in unnecessary costs.

C. REMITTANCES AND DIASPORA BONDS

Migration is a wide-spread phenomenon in Africa. Many Africans have migrated to other African countries or beyond. While living abroad, many migrants continue supporting their families with their savings and by sending remittances home. Remittances have grown remarkably over the last 15 years and provided financial support to countless families. At the same time and recognizing the scope and stability of these flows, Governments and financial institutions have designed financial instruments to tap diaspora savings and leverage remittances for development finance.

According to World Bank estimates remittances to developing countries stood at $436 billion in 2014, a 4.4 per cent increase over 2013; it forecasts an increase to $479 billion by 2017 (World Bank, 2015c). In Africa, remittances were estimated at $63.8 billion in 2014, surpassing both official development assistance and foreign direct investment flows to the continent. Growth in remittances to Africa in 2014 largely reflected strong growth in Kenya (10.7 per cent), South Africa (7 per cent) and Uganda (6.7 per cent). While remittances are highly concentrated in Africa, with Nigeria accounting for 33 per cent; Egypt, 31 per cent; and Morocco, 11 per cent, they are crucial for several other African countries in terms of their contribution to GDP and/or as a source of foreign exchange. Table 8 shows that smaller States and non-oil producers, such as Cabo Verde, the Comoros, the Gambia, Lesotho, Liberia and Senegal, tend to be more dependent on remittance flows.

This section discusses how remittances and diaspora savings can contribute to public and development finance. As the potential of remittances for development finance greatly depends on the use of official channels, the section looks at how official channels can be encouraged. Finally, it shows how remittances and diaspora bonds relate to public debt.

Leveraging remittances and diaspora savings for development finance

The savings and savings potential of diasporas are sizeable. World Bank (2015c) estimates suggest that the annual savings of diasporas from developing countries,

Table 8.   Remittances as a share of gross domestic product, exports, official development assistance and foreign direct investment, average of 2011–2013 (Percentage)

	GDP	Exports	ODA	FDI
Algeria	1	2.6	1 098.8	70.9
Angola	0	0	0	0
Benin	2.5	15.8	31.9	78.2
Botswana	0.2	0.3	25	3.3
Burkina Faso	1.1	4.8	11.4	37.5
Burundi	1.9	18.8	8.5	1 301.3
Cabo Verde	9.7	28.3	71.4	179.7
Cameroon	0.8	4.2	34.5	44.8
Comoros	18.8	119.3	167.5	779
Côte d'Ivoire	1.3	2.8	21	107.8
Democratic Republic of the Congo	0.2	0.5	1.5	2.3
Djibouti	2.5	7.6	23.2	21.3
Egypt	6.7	37.3	665	527.7
Ethiopia	1.4	10.5	16.6	94.8
Gambia	15.9	79.5	110.6	217.9
Ghana	0.3	0.7	8.3	4.2
Guinea	1.3	4.8	22	13.2
Guinea-Bissau	4.8	23	47.4	279.5
Kenya	2.4	12.1	41.3	317.2
Lesotho	23.6	52	195.8	993.3
Liberia	24.1	84.1	67.6	44.5
Madagascar	4	14.3	92.7	55.8
Malawi	0.6	1.8	2.6	21.7
Mali	7.8	29.8	68.5	198.6
Mauritius	2.2	4	145.5	58.3
Morocco	6.9	19.7	421	240.2
Mozambique	1.4	4.8	9.2	3.9
Namibia	0.1	0.2	5	1.5
Niger	2.2	10	20.1	17.9
Nigeria	4.5	16.9	1 003.8	287
Rwanda	2.5	18.2	16.3	83.4
Sao Tome and Principe	4.8	36.9	23	60.8
Senegal	11.2	41	155.2	523
Seychelles	1.5	1.8	67.2	8.7
Sierra Leone	1.6	4.8	14.3	14.2
South Africa	0.3	0.9	85.5	18.8
Sudan	0.6	44.3	27.5	21.1
Swaziland	0.9	1.5	30.3	44.6
Togo	8.4	19.7	100.3	99.4
Tunisia	4.7	10	247.7	169.6
Uganda	4	17.6	54.1	83.2
United Republic of Tanzania	0.2	0.9	2.4	4
Zambia	0.2	0.6	5.5	3.2
Median	2.2	10	31.9	58.3

Source: UNCTAD secretariat calculations, based on data from IMF, OECD International Development Statistics online databases, UNCTAD, 2016 and the World Bank.

Note: Sample size of 43 countries. Remittances, GDP, exports (including goods and services), official development assistance (ODA) and foreign direct investment (FDI) are current prices and averages for 2011–2013.

estimated by using data on international migrants, amounted to $497 billion in 2013. A large part of these savings is used for remittances to home countries. Once they are consumed and spent in the recipient country, remittances contribute to government budgets through indirect taxation.

A large share of diaspora savings is held in bank deposits. As deposits held in host-country banks currently receive near-zero interest rates, migrant workers may find it attractive to invest their savings in other outlets or vehicles. One such outlet is diaspora bonds: "debt instruments issued by a sovereign country to raise funds by placing them among its diaspora population" (UNCTAD, 2012b). Diaspora bonds may also benefit from emotional connections or patriotic motives to attract investment, which can make them less procyclical than other external capital flows. It is crucial for Governments considering the emission of diaspora bonds to determine whether the cost of capital acquired through diaspora bonds is lower than the cost of capital raised in international capital markets. For countries with little or no access to international capital markets, this issue is, however, irrelevant, as these bonds may be the only alternative to raising foreign currency other than through exports. Furthermore, the costs of marketing and retailing diaspora bonds can be substantial and may offset the benefits of the lower interest rates paid to bond holders. To reach a sufficient number of migrants and thus reduce the cost of issuing such bonds, UNCTAD (2012) proposed a regional issuance of diaspora bonds by a group of countries supported by a regional development bank.

Several countries have been very successful in placing diaspora bonds. For example, the Development Corporation for Israel has raised over $25 billion since 1951, and the State Bank of India, over $11 billion since 1991 (Ketkar and Ratha, 2010). Sri Lanka Development Bonds have raised about $580 million since 2001. According to the World Bank (2015c), diaspora bonds could be used to mobilize about one tenth of the annual diaspora savings – over $50 billion – to finance development projects.

Some African countries – Ethiopia, Ghana, Kenya and Zimbabwe, for example – are also exploring the option of issuing diaspora bonds to bridge financing gaps. In 2007, the Government of Ghana issued a $50 million Golden Jubilee savings bond targeted at Ghanaians at home and abroad. The funds raised through the sale of the bonds would be invested in infrastructure projects in Ghana. In 2011, Ethiopia launched its second diaspora bond, the Renaissance Dam Bond, the proceeds of which were used to fund the construction of the Grand Renaissance Dam at an estimated cost of $4.8 billion (African Development Bank, 2012). The Renaissance

Dam bond was based on the concept of a patriotic discount (a benefit to the issuer), which refers to a diaspora bond coupon level that is lower than the benchmark, typically the 10-year United States treasury bond or other comparable bonds. Therefore, the purchase of the diaspora bond is at a premium and is dependent on an emotional connection with the issuing country (UNCTAD, 2012b).

The African experience with diaspora bonds suggests that they tend to do better where a receiving country has a sizeable first-generation diaspora in middle-to high-income countries. Therefore, countries such as Egypt, Ethiopia, Kenya, Nigeria, Somalia and South Africa, and those with a large proportion of their population abroad, should be well placed to benefit from a strong diaspora bond policy. But some African countries might not be able to attract investors because of a perception of political risk. They may also struggle to harness the potential of diaspora bonds because of technical or bureaucratic requirements for selling them abroad, for example in the United States.

Another option for attracting diaspora members to invest their savings in their home countries are foreign-currency-denominated bank deposits offered by financial institutions in home countries. Such deposits eliminate the foreign currency risk, which is a component of the risk premium of the home country. At the same time, the remainder of the risk premium will ensure that the return on savings is still higher than the return on savings offered by bank deposits in most host countries. These accounts are attractive, particularly for longer term two- or three-year deposits, owing to the higher interest rates they can offer. Moreover, they strengthen the balance sheets of home country banks and encourage the financial deepening of the economy.

As remittance flows have proved relatively stable over the medium to long term, they can serve as future-flow receivables for securitization. There have been examples of the use of future remittances for securitization to lower interest rates and extend debt maturity. According to Ketkar and Ratha (2009), Banco do Brasil raised $250 million in 2002 through a bond securitized by future flows of remittances from Japan. The bond had a higher credit rating than Brazil's sovereign rating (BBB+ versus BB-) and its interest rate was about 9 percentage points lower than the sovereign borrowing rate. The requirements for this instrument are, however, stringent: in general, countries must have a credit rating of B or above, receive a minimum of $500 million per year in remittances and allow a few banks to handle the majority of the remittance flows.

Compared with the securitization of bonds, less stringent conditions apply for using remittances as collateral for long-term syndicated loans.[39] Sovereign risk can be mitigated by remittances, and development banks can offer credit enhancement instruments. The African Export-Import Bank has experience in arranging remittance-based future-flow syndicated loans. In 2001, it launched its Financial Future-Flow Pre-Financing Programme to expand the use of remittances and other future flows as collateral to leverage external financing at lower costs and longer maturities. In 2013, 5 per cent of its loans emanated from that Programme. It has led to various future-remittance-flow collateral-backed loans in Ethiopia, Ghana and Nigeria. The Bank has received awards for such activities, since they have enhanced the access of African counterparties to reasonably priced external trade and project financing from the markets using remittances by Africans in the diaspora as collateral and as the main source of repayment (UNCTAD, 2012b).

The use of remittances for financial deepening and as collateral for loans or securitization is subject to remittances being officially recorded. This means that remittances must be transferred through formal channels. However, migrants generally utilize a whole range of formal and informal channels for remitting, chosen on the basis of cost, reliability, accessibility and trust. As a result, a large share of remittances is transmitted through informal channels and thus remains unrecorded.

Encouraging formal remittance channels

Policies for encouraging formal remittance channels should address the factors that make informal networks attractive, that is, in particular, lower costs of remitting and greater availability of services, especially in rural areas.

Reducing remittance costs should be facilitated through policies in sending and receiving countries. UNCTAD (2012) notes that for reducing remittance costs in many sending countries, "a key prerequisite is the regularization of the status of migrants and their eligibility to open bank accounts". If migrants could utilize the host country's financial services for transferring remittances, the larger volume of remittances would work as an incentive for other players in the financial sector to enter the remittance market. This would lead to greater competition and therefore lower remittance costs.

In recipient countries, there is a tendency to increase competition of service providers. In many least developed countries in Africa, formal remittance channels are controlled by a small number of such service providers. This practice of exclusive agreements stifles competition by preventing competitors from entering the market and results in high fees and fewer service providers. Exclusivity agreements should thus be revised; so should regulations on money transfers and supervision of financial institutions to allow, for instance, microfinance institutions, savings and loan cooperatives, credit unions and post offices to be more active in remittance channels (Maimbo and Ratha, 2005; Orozco and Fedewa, 2006). This would reduce the costs of remitting and ensure greater rural penetration.

UNCTAD (2012) stresses that "promoting competition raises regulatory issues, primarily the need to ensure the reliability and integrity of the transfer systems and to avoid the system being abused (for example for money laundering)". The latter stresses the need for policymakers to strike a balance between promoting competition in this market and maintaining supportive regulations.

Furthermore, recipient countries can improve the attractiveness of formal channels by enabling diaspora members to open foreign-currency-denominated bank accounts in home countries, which eliminate the foreign currency risk. For instance, the National Bank of Ethiopia in 2004 allowed Ethiopians abroad and foreign nationals of Ethiopian origin to open foreign-currency accounts in any of the authorized commercial banks in the country.

There is scope for a greater use of new technologies, particularly Internet-based and mobile telephony-driven methods of transmitting funds, which have created opportunities for branchless banking and improved rural access to financial services.

Facilitating and increasing the use of formal remittance channels is central to the African Institute for Remittances, led by the African Union with the support of the World Bank and the European Commission, and in cooperation with the African Development Bank and the International Organization for Migration. The Institute aims to facilitate cheaper, faster and more secure remittance flows from Europe to Africa, and to build the capacity of African Union Member States, remittance senders and recipients, and other stakeholders to develop and implement sound strategies and operational instruments to use remittances as development tools for poverty reduction.[40]

Impact of remittances and diaspora bonds on public debt

Remittances relate to public debt in several ways. First, remittances (worker remittances and employee compensation) make a positive contribution to the current account of the balance of payments. In deficit-driven economies, remittances thus ease the balance-of-payments gap and result in less need for debt to finance the deficit. Second, IMF and the World Bank have gradually moved towards a revision of the Debt Sustainability Framework so as to account for the impact of remittances on the debt repayment capacity as well as on the probability of default (IMF and World Bank, 2012; World Bank and IMF, 2014). When sound remittance data are available, such data are used to assess the risk of debt distress. Third, as remittances increase the level and often the stability of foreign exchange receipts and thus have a positive impact on the recipient country's ability to repay its external debt, the creditworthiness of the recipient country is improved. Better credit ratings will result in lower borrowing costs. Fourth, and as discussed above, when remittances serve as collateral for securitization or long-term syndicated loans, they can reduce the costs Governments face in international capital markets and potentially broaden access to long-term development finance. Through diaspora bonds, Governments can increase their development finance options and borrow at interest rates that are usually lower than in domestic markets and possibly also lower than in international capital markets when emotional and patriotic motives drive investment.

Remittances and diaspora bonds create significant foreign currency inflows that require careful macroeconomic management, especially of the exchange rate (Ratha and Plaza, 2011) and of the extent to which recipients have sufficient capacity to absorb and spend or invest resources. In some countries, these inflows may bear the risk of currency appreciation (Ratha, 2013). This also applies to bonds that are issued in domestic currency, as they generate large foreign currency inflows after a bond issuance and potential outflows when the bond matures.

D. CURTAILING ILLICIT FINANCIAL FLOWS

Every year large amounts of money are transferred out of Africa illegally. Illicit financial flows have a damaging impact on the countries. They limit resources needed for domestic expenditure and public and private investment and may undermine governance, while facilitating transnational organized crime and fostering corruption. Illicit financial flows and their costs to African economies are thus a development issue of major concern for policymakers. Many damaging capital (out)flows are not illegal, depending on legislative contexts and are beyond the regulatory capacity of most economies to capture, for example offshore tax havens. However, they may be at least as significant, if not more so, than illicit financial flows and therefore of relevance in the wider context of development finance.

According to the 2014 Report of the High-level Panel on Illicit Financial Flows from Africa, illicit financial flows can be as high as $50 billion per year. It is estimated that Africa lost about $854 billion in illicit financial flows between 1970 and 2008, which corresponds on average to $22 billion per year. This sum is nearly equivalent to all official development assistance received by Africa in that time frame (OECD, 2015b), and only a third of it would have been enough to fully cover its external debt, which reached $279 billion in 2008. Data from Global Financial Integrity suggest that over the period 2002–2011, illicit financial flows in Africa were the second fastest growing of all regions, at a rate of 19.8 per cent per year, and the highest as a share of GDP, at 5.7 per cent (Herkenrath, 2014). While estimates differ according to the method used, the Panel notes that estimates by Ndikumana and Boyce (2008; 2011), Kar and Cartwright-Smith (2010) and Kar and Freitas (2011), all point to two important findings: illicit financial flows are high for Africa; and illicit financial flows from the continent have been increasing over time.

In a time of urgent need for financing for development, serious considerations should be given to the way illicit financial flows can be substantially reduced to augment domestic financial resources. This is recognized in the Addis Ababa Action Agenda of the Third International Conference on Financing for Development (A/RES/69/313), endorsed by the international community in 2015. In the context of domestic public resources, it states: "We will redouble efforts to substantially reduce illicit financial flows by 2030, with a view to eventually eliminating them, including by combating tax evasion and corruption through strengthened national regulation and increased international cooperation".

Overall, African countries have two interrelated objectives: to redouble efforts aimed at domestic resource mobilization, including by stemming illicit financial flows, and to engage in a range of policy reforms to attract private capital, while ensuring that it is channelled towards structural transformation and preventing illicit financial flows.

Illicit financial flows and how they take place

Global Financial Integrity defines illicit financial flows as "illegal movements of money or capital from one country to another" and classifies this movement as an illicit flow when the funds are illegally earned, transferred, and/or utilized. This is also the definition adopted by the Panel, noting that "these flows of money are in violation of laws in their origin, or during their movement or use, and are therefore considered illicit". Furthermore, it stresses the importance of distinguishing illicit financial flows from capital flight, which can be driven by macroeconomic and governance factors and be entirely licit.

Illicit financial flows have three main components. Some distinguish between commercial (trade-related) activities, criminal activities and corruption (Global Financial Integrity), while others classify illicit financial flows as proceeds of criminal activities, corruption and tax evasion, including abusive transfer pricing (Task Force on Development Impact of Illicit Financial Flows, 2011). Given the scope of this report, the focus is on the commercial component of illicit financial flows that arise from business-related activities. The Panel notes that these flows have several purposes, "including hiding wealth, evading or aggressively avoiding tax, and dodging customs duties and domestic levies", and that "these are complex to determine in terms of the dividing line between the fair use of policy incentives and their abuse and the range and scope of economic activities from which such outflows can emanate". The challenge lies in determining and identifying transactions that constitute tax evasion (illegal) and those that constitute tax avoidance (legal, if not abusive, tax avoidance).

According to the High-level Panel on Illicit Financial Flows from Africa, illicit financial flows relating to commercial activities, that is, tax evasion, can take place through various means:

- Transfer mispricing is the manipulation of prices of cross-border transactions between related multinational corporations. If they use their multiple structures to shift profits across different jurisdictions without applying the arm's-length principle, they engage in base erosion and profit shifting. These are particularly complicated to detect, given the complex international production networks;

- Trade mispricing is the falsification of the price, quality and quantity values of traded goods for a variety of purposes. Practices include the underinvoicing of exports and the overinvoicing of imports;

- Misinvoicing of services and intangibles are often connected to intra-group loans and intellectual property and management fees. This type of illicit financial flow is supported by changing technology and a lack of comparative price information;

- Unequal contracts refer to contracts that are concluded in secrecy and fuelled by bribes to circumvent existing legal provisions. Such contracts are often of concern in the extractive industries. A further concern therein is the asymmetry of information between countries and multinational corporations, which often have more information about the quantity and quality of mineral deposits for which contracts are being signed.

Kar and Cartwright-Smith (2010) estimate that the proceeds of commercial tax evasion, mainly through trade mispricing, are by far the largest component, at some 60–65 per cent of the global total. This signals the importance of dialogue and cooperation between the State and the private sector, as well as the pursuit of corporate governance when implementing measures to tackle the problem.

Economic implications of illicit financial flows

Illicit financial flows directly undermine efforts to mobilize domestic resources. They reduce the estimated gains from deliberate national policies that could be put in place to strengthen domestic resource mobilization, particularly through tax and public administration reforms, governance reforms, financial development and from harnessing benefits from remittances. Therefore, tackling illicit financial flows is imperative if African countries wish to successfully strengthen domestic resource mobilization.

Illicit financial flows also impose indirect costs by, for instance, blunting incentives for corrupt government officials and private players to engage in and support structural transformation aimed at reducing dependence on extractive industries. The High-level Panel on Illicit Financial Flows from Africa noted, for instance, that such flows were highest in the extractive industries, especially oil, precious metals and minerals, iron and steel and copper. Illicit financial flows may blunt incentives for pro-development governance reforms and capacity development that are likely to be resisted by powerful private and public interest groups benefiting from illicit activities. Such flows may also undermine the building of political institutions and contribute to preserving unequal power relations in society, with negative impacts on social and economic development (Herkenrath, 2014). Public and private investment decisions are often distorted, with adverse consequences on the return of investment. For example, corrupt officials are likely to divert investment to economic sectors that are more conducive to bribery rather than to sectors that matter more for structural transformation. Illicit financial flows deepen inequality, as this practice is mostly carried out by elites who engage in trade mispricing of exports and imports, or those with the power to unlawfully appropriate or transfer resources abroad (African Development Bank et al., 2012).

Moreover, illicit financial flows reinforce the dependence of countries on aid and external debt. However, as previously stated, such dependence is not sustainable, While aid is often unpredictable and volatile, and is not desirable for long-term use as a financing modality, dependence on external debt incurs risks for debt sustainability, and aid and external debt reduce the policy space of African countries.

Combating illicit financial flows

Financial flows that result from corruption and criminal activities are illegal in nature and should be tackled first through better governance. While these issues are important, they go beyond the scope of this report. This report focuses on how illicit financial flows evolving from commercial activities (tax evasion) can be combated and how opportunities for tax avoidance can be reduced to enhance value retention in countries of origin. Tax administrators face major challenges in detecting illicit outflows that occur through sophisticated tax avoidance schemes involving transfer-pricing mechanisms, the exploitation of loopholes in tax laws and the financial secrecy offered by tax havens to multinational corporations and wealthy individuals. Clearly, these issues require action at both the national and international levels.

National level

The Panel recognizes the importance of a clear regulatory framework that makes it "illegal to intentionally[,] incorrectly or inaccurately state the price, quantity, quality or other aspect of trade in goods and services in order to move capital or profits to another jurisdiction or to manipulate, evade or avoid any form of taxation including customs and excise duties". The framework is credible and effective when enforcement mechanisms are introduced to administer punishment to those who infringe regulations.

An efficient and effective customs administration is essential to curtail trade misinvoicing. Countries should boost their customs enforcement by equipping and training officers to better detect the intentional misinvoicing of transactions. The Automated System for Customs Data, or ASYCUDA, can be a useful tool in this regard. It aims at increasing customs revenue by ensuring that all goods are declared, that duty and tax calculations are correct and that duties, exemptions, preference regimes and the like are correctly applied and managed. Overall, ASYCUDA is designed to reform and speed up the customs clearance process by introducing computerization and simplifying procedures, thus minimizing administrative costs to the business community and the economies of countries.

The Panel also recommends that national and multilateral agencies make fully and freely available, and in a timely manner, data on pricing of goods and services in international transactions, according to accepted coding categories. Using such databases will enable countries to compare prices and identify transactions that require additional scrutiny. Furthermore, countries should build their own databases to create a more robust data set of local and regional comparators.

Tax collection greatly depends on the capacity of tax administration. Countries should establish transfer-pricing units that are well equipped in accordance with global best practices and are situated in revenue authorities. Multinational corporations operating in a country should be required to disclose or provide to these units their revenues, profits, losses, sales, taxes paid, subsidiaries and staff levels country by country or subsidiary by subsidiary. Furthermore, trade transactions involving tax haven jurisdictions should be treated with the highest level of scrutiny by customs, tax and law enforcement officials (Spanjers and Frede Foss, 2015).

The Panel also recommends that countries establish or strengthen the independent institutions and agencies of Government responsible for preventing illicit financial flows, including methods and mechanisms for information sharing and coordination among key stakeholders. As banks and financial institutions have a major role in preventing and eliminating illicit financial flows, they should be supervised by central banks and financial supervision agencies through robust regimes. Financial regulators should require that all banks in their country know the true beneficial owner(s) of any account opened in their financial institutions.

International level

African countries will not be able to successfully combat illicit financial flows without stronger and more committed cooperation from their regional and international partners.

At the global level, there has been an important push for international cooperation in tax matters. The Global Forum on Transparency and Exchange of Information for Tax Purposes, working under the auspices of OECD and the Group of 20, has been the multilateral framework within which work on transparency and the exchange of information for tax purposes has been carried out by both OECD and non-OECD countries since 2000. Following restructuring in 2009, the Global Forum became the international body that ensures that international standards on transparency and the exchange of information for tax purposes are in place around the world through its monitoring and peer-review activities.

The Base Erosion and Profit Shifting Project of OECD and the Group of 20, endorsed by finance ministers of the Group in July 2013, recommended that taxation and economic activities be realigned, that coherence between national tax systems be ensured and that enhanced transparency be promoted. At a meeting of the Group in Brisbane, Australia, in November 2014, leaders endorsed the Common Reporting Standard for the automatic exchange of tax information and agreed to begin exchanging information with each other and with other countries by 2017 or the end of 2018, subject to the completion of necessary legislative procedures. While all countries are invited to join the new standards, it is acknowledged that some developing countries face serious capacity constraints to their implementation. The Global Forum provides capacity-building ranging from skills support activities to peer-to-peer learning between member jurisdictions and the development of tools that support the implementation of the standards.

In line with this framework, ministers and other representatives of African countries launched the African Initiative to increase awareness of the merits of transparency. The project is led by African members of the Global Forum and the Chair and Co-founder of the African Tax Administration Forum, in collaboration with the Forum, OECD, the World Bank Group and the *Centre de rencontres et d'études des dirigeants des administrations fiscales.*

Emanating from OECD work on harmful tax practices, tax information exchange agreements were developed in 2002. The OECD Committee on Fiscal Affairs in June 2015 approved a model protocol to these agreements. Through this protocol, jurisdictions can extend the scope of their existing agreements on the exchange of information on tax matters to also cover the automatic and/or spontaneous exchange of information. Low-income countries face, however, significant challenges in making use of such agreements. As they are bilateral agreements, these countries have neither the capacity nor the political influence to secure large numbers of tax information exchange agreements; further, such agreements are based on requests for information exchange, which means the process of accessing information from tax havens through a tax information exchange agreement is difficult and time consuming. Africa's regional integration has a role to play in this process. For example, the East African Community has developed a code of conduct to prevent harmful tax competition and promote the harmonization of tax incentives, avoiding beggar-thy-neighbour and race to-the-bottom corporate tax incentive policies.

A significant component of trade-related illicit financial flows occurs either through trade mispricing, transfer pricing or base erosion and profit shifting practised by multinational corporations (African Union and United Nations Economic Commission for Africa Conference of Ministers of Finance, Planning and Economic Development, 2014; Economic Justice Network, 2011). Multinational corporations are increasingly urged to apply a country-by-country reporting accounting standard, which requires them to report to tax authorities disaggregated details of investment, employment, revenue, profit and tax in each jurisdiction where they do business.

To promote coherence between international tax and investment policies, UNCTAD (2015d) proposed the following 10 principles and guidelines:

- Tolerance or facilitation of tax avoidance should not be considered an instrument to attract inward investment or to support the competitiveness of multinational enterprises abroad;

- It is important to mitigate the impact on investment of anti-avoidance measures;

- National investment policymakers should consider options at the entry and establishment levels to prevent tax avoidance;

- Investment promotion and facilitation options and constructive relationship management with investors can be leveraged to reduce the motivation and opportunity for tax avoidance;

- Any national or international action to tackle tax avoidance should consider interdependencies with international investment agreements;

- International investment agreements and double taxation treaties are both part of countries' investment facilitation toolkits; these instruments should be aligned;

- Policymakers should recognize the role in cross-border corporate tax avoidance played by different types of offshore investment hubs as well as by home and host countries; they should clarify shared responsibility and take comprehensive action;

- Tax avoidance and the lack of transparency in international financial transactions are global issues that require a multilateral approach, with adequate developing-country participation;

- Policymakers should consider the importance of international investment and tax revenues for sustainable development finance, and the specific features of tax avoidance in developing countries;

- Investment and ownership information is key to analysing tax-avoidance schemes and should be prioritized, together with other tools, to enable anti-avoidance measures and foster good tax behaviour.

Regulations should also be developed to cater for more effective disclosure and transparency practices in the banking sector. The Economic Development in Africa Report 2015 highlighted this problem and a lack of adequate prudential regulation, especially given the rise of cross-border banking. Foreign banks accounted for over 52 per cent of all commercial banks in Africa in 2009, and 58 per cent of total bank assets. Key problems include the lack of harmonized banking supervision standards and requirements across jurisdictions, and regulatory skills shortages, leading to a lack of capability to supervise across borders or across financial services subsectors, or to maintain oversight of outsourced activities.

Greater advocacy is needed on the part of the African Union and the United Nations to raise awareness of African Governments, African academics, non-governmental organizations and other civil society bodies about the need to translate the recommendations of the High-level Panel on Illicit Financial Flows from Africa into tangible actions at the national and regional levels, as follows:

- Multilaterally, under the auspices of the African Union and the United Nations, a recurrent forum could be organized to bring together African States and developed countries to debate on how international cooperation should be harnessed and how an international framework could be established to combat illicit financial flows. For example, this could be accomplished by producing an international register of multinational corporations with details on their operations and accounts, and by introducing universally comparable information disclosure requirements on multinational corporations. Governments from other regions could also be invited to these forums in order to highlight the global dimension of the problem and the need for global cooperation and coordination;

- At the bilateral level, African States should approach their development partners for technical assistance on how to deal with the causes and symptoms of illicit financial flows. This could be achieved, for example, by addressing trade mispricing through the introduction of automated customs systems that allow importing and exporting countries to compare swiftly the value, quality and quantity of tradable goods and exchange information; by providing assistance to set up units to combat illicit financial flows; and by fostering cooperation across such units across countries.

Given that illicit financial flows are a global problem, the experience of the Panel could contribute to a global architecture or governance structure that tackles them more effectively if they are addressed in a frank and open dialogue that contextualizes them in the broader setting of development and, ultimately, development finance.

Moreover, interrelated initiatives such as the Africa Mining Vision, the Extractive Industries Transparency Initiative, the Financial Action Task Force and the Stolen Asset Recovery Initiative[41] should be fully brought on board to avoid duplication while leveraging on their experiences and best practices. Although not addressed in the Addis Ababa Action Agenda, the problem of illicit financial flows is inextricably linked to illegitimate and odious debts, and decisive actions are needed to put an end to their reaccumulation (box 7). Lastly, the vital role of civil society as a watchdog of transparency should be recognized and used as an additional layer of vigilance.

Box 7. Addressing odious debt

The legal doctrine of odious debt argues that sovereign debt incurred without the consent of the people and not benefiting them is odious and should not be transferable to a successor Government, especially if creditors are aware of these facts. According to Howse (2007), the concept of odious debt regroups a particular set of equitable considerations that have often been raised to adjust or sever debt obligations in the context of political transitions. A survey of such transitional situations indicates that where odiousness is argued as grounds for limiting obligations, it varies from one transitional context to another, depending on whether it involves a secession, arises from war or decolonization or is simply a political revolution.

Kremer and Jayachandran (2002) suggest two mechanisms to ensure that lending to odious regimes is eliminated. First, laws in creditor countries could be changed to disallow the seizure of a country's assets for non-repayment of odious debt. That is, odious debt contracts could be made legally unenforceable. Second, foreign aid to successor regimes could be made contingent on the non-repayment of odious debt. In other words, donors could refuse to aid a country that, in effect, was handing funds over to banks with illegitimate claims.

CHAPTER **5**
MAIN FINDINGS AND
POLICY RECOMMENDATIONS

Africa's multiple development aspirations face major challenges: enormous financing requirements in a changing financing landscape and rapidly rising public debt. As the continent embarks on its economic transformation agenda, the role of domestic debt is becoming increasingly important. In harnessing the various development finance resources, African countries will need to strike a balance between increased financing needs and overall debt sustainability.

This report has examined some of the key policy issues that underlie Africa's domestic and external debt and provides policy guidance on the delicate balancing between financing development alternatives and overall debt sustainability considerations. This chapter recapitulates some of the main findings, key messages and policy recommendations of the report.

A. MAIN FINDINGS

The main findings of the report are as follows:

- *Africa faces major challenges in meeting its development finance needs through public budgetary resources.*

  It is estimated that financing the Sustainable Development Goals in Africa could require investments of between $600 billion and $1.2 trillion per year (Chinzana et al., 2015; Schmidt-Traub, 2015; UNCTAD, 2014). Infrastructure alone would cost $93 billion, but Africa can only raise half of this amount.

- *External debt in Africa is on the rise and is mainly related to reduced export revenues, a widening current account deficit and slower economic growth.*

  In 2011–2013, the external debt stock amounted on average to $443 billion, compared with $303 billion in 2006–2009. Ratios of external debt to GNI are low, at less than 40 per cent in most African countries. While the combined stock of external debt fell over time – from 107 per cent of GNI in 2000 – several African countries have experienced an upward trend. However, these broad trends in absolute terms disguise the rapid rise of external debt levels in several African countries in recent years. Although debt–GNI ratios have not changed much since 2006, the external debt stock grew rapidly by an average 10.2 per cent per year in 2011–2013, compared with 7.8 per cent in 2006–2009. The main drivers of this debt accumulation are associated with a growing current account deficit and slower economic growth.

- *The composition, terms and conditions of external debt are changing.*

  First, the share of concessional financing[42] declined in two thirds of the heavily indebted poor countries in Africa from 2005–2007 to 2011–2013. Second, these countries have experienced a marked, steady decline in the maturity and grace period of new external debt commitments on average since 2005. The average interest on their new external debt commitments has also worsened, although it remained below the average for non-heavily indebted poor countries in Africa, as well as for low-income countries. Third, public and publicly guaranteed debt from private creditors has not only risen in both heavily indebted poor countries and non-heavily indebted poor countries, but has also become more diversified. A lower share of concessional debt, higher interest rates, lower maturities and grace periods are most likely to increase the debt burden of African countries.

- *The structure and composition of debt matters for debt sustainability and the Debt Sustainability Framework.*

  The joint World Bank–IMF Debt Sustainability Framework for Low-income Countries is designed to help low-income countries achieve debt sustainability on their new borrowing from concessional official loans. The main rationale for the framework is to assess the sustainability of debt to avoid risks related to debt distress. The current framework needs to be revisited to prevent low-income countries from becoming locked into a low-debt low-growth scenario, and it should also reflect domestic debt exposure in its debt sustainability analysis. Maintaining external debt sustainability is a challenge for African countries in their efforts to finance national development strategies and in the context of the 2030 Agenda for Sustainable Development.

- *Domestic debt is growing gradually and increasingly consists of marketable debt.*

  The stylized facts emerging from the data analysis of five case studies reveal the gradual increase in domestic debt, from an average of 11 per cent of GDP in 1995 to 17 per cent of GDP in 2014. Furthermore, most Governments have increasingly met funding requirements through marketable debt, as opposed to non-marketable debt. Marketable securities include commercial paper, bankers' acceptances, treasury bills and other monetary market instruments.

- *Domestic capital markets have been deepening as international investor interest has grown.*

  More and more countries have achieved the capacity to issue local-currency-denominated debt securities of long maturities over the past decade, suggesting that the problem of original sin could be gradually dissipating. In general, market depth has increased, maturities have lengthened and the investor base has broadened, making domestic borrowing much easier for Governments in the context of the global financial cycle that has led international financial investors to access markets that they had considered too risky in the past. Nevertheless, there is scope for further strengthening of the functioning of the existing domestic debt markets, including through a reform of the non-banking financial sector to widen the investor base for long-dated government securities. Further strengthening of the retirement benefits industry and the insurance sector could increase the amount of long-term savings available for the domestic debt markets. Although the interest burden of domestic debt is still higher than that of external debt, there is evidence that this is declining over time, in line with deepening domestic debt markets. However, external debt has foreign exchange risks to which domestic debt is not exposed; therefore, the interest cost on local-currency-denominated domestic debt should not be viewed as the only deciding factor for the use of domestic debt markets to raise resources for financing development. Rather, the risk–return profile of domestic and external debt instruments should also be considered. Lastly, the dynamic effects of financial deepening should not be underestimated in the context of pro-poor growth and transformative economic development, as financial deepening can greatly affect the provision of access to financial services for the unbanked, especially women – only 20 per cent of women have access to formal financial services in Africa (UNCTAD, 2015c).

- *Public–private partnerships are spreading and warrant caution from a debt-management perspective.*

  Compared with other geographical regions, infrastructure public–private partnerships in Africa are smaller in magnitude and number, but they are increasing. Public–private partnerships, especially those involved in infrastructure development, are complex undertakings with considerable risks. They are generally capital-intensive, long-term projects with complex contractual arrangements that make their proper evaluation and recording a challenge. Thus, setting up a public–private partnership policy framework that addresses and mitigates these risks is essential and requires a broad set of legal, managerial and technical capacities. A considerable risk of such partnerships relates to their treatment as off-budget transactions (contingent liabilities) and they can become a fiscal burden in the future. This treatment may also encourage countries to use them in order to circumvent national or IMF-agreed debt limits. Estimates of the impact of contingent liabilities on debt sustainability are not included in the current debt sustainability framework.

- *Remittances and diaspora savings are an opportunity for development finance.*

Governments and financial institutions have designed financial instruments to tap diaspora savings and leverage remittances for development finance. The interest rate applied to diaspora bonds should be attractive to foreign investors to compensate for the political risk. Issuer countries might also struggle to tap the potential of diaspora bonds, owing to technical or bureaucratic requirements concerning their sale abroad. The use of formal remittance channels should be encouraged so that remittances can serve as collateral and lead to financial deepening.

- *Illicit financial flows could become a source of development finance, as long as efforts to tackle them at the national and international levels are sustained.*

Africa needs continued continent-wide cooperation, and engagement and support from international organizations and their members in tackling illicit financial flows and debt relief. This is crucial, as Africa lost about $854 billion in such flows from 1970 to 2008. This sum is nearly equivalent to all official development assistance received during that period and only one third would have been sufficient to cover its external debt.

- On a global scale, the experience of the High-level Panel on Illicit Financial Flows from Africa could contribute to a global architecture or governance structure that combats illicit financial flows more effectively if such flows are addressed in a frank and open dialogue that contextualizes illicit financial flows in the broader setting of development, and ultimately development finance. It is imperative that all stakeholders interact and form part of this dialogue. Moreover, initiatives such as the Africa Mining Vision, the Extractive Industries Transparency Initiative, the Financial Action Task Force, the Global

Forum on Transparency and Exchange of Information for Tax Purposes and the Stolen Asset Recovery Initiative should be fully brought on board to avoid duplication while leveraging on their experiences and best practices. Lastly, the vital role of civil society in monitoring transparency should be recognized and used to provide additional vigilance.

B. MAIN POLICY RECOMMENDATIONS

Africa is at a critical juncture in its development. As a result of the high costs of financing the Sustainable Development Goals, which are unlikely to be covered by official development assistance and external debt alone, the importance of domestic debt in development finance has gained prominence. However, this also highlights the importance of maintaining debt sustainability and preventing debt distress. Clearly, achieving the Goals and maintaining debt sustainability is desirable. The difficult question is how African countries may achieve the dual goal of covering their development finance needs and maintaining debt sustainability. This section therefore discusses some key policy recommendations that may help Africa in this endeavour.

1. *Raise adequate levels of financing for development from domestic and external sources to meet development goals and achieve structural transformation*

Given the complexity of Africa's development challenges, the scale of its development finance needs and the severity of its capacity constraints, African countries need to leverage all possible sources of finance. Debt, both domestic and external, as well as other complementary sources, cannot be excluded from Africa's list of development finance policy options. Therefore, debt channelled to investments for Sustainable Development Goals should be afforded more flexibility. For example, if debt is channelled to building resilience (Goal 9), this could contribute to lifting major productive capacity constraints, and thereby spur structural transformation. However, most of the investments needed for reaching the Goals cannot be financed through debt alone, as this would affect debt sustainability for most African States. Domestic resource mobilization for investment in the building of productive capacities will be key for Africa's structural transformation (UNCTAD, 2015e).

2. *Leverage domestic and external debt without compromising debt sustainability*

Debt sustainability is never guaranteed. Any severe shock may push a given country over the limits of sustainable debt. It would not make sense to restrict new borrowing so drastically solely to guarantee long-term debt sustainability. A better balance must be reached between the benefits of new concessional and non-concessional borrowing from domestic and external sources and the benefits of restricting any such borrowing to achieve debt sustainability. Therefore, Africa needs to continue strengthening macroeconomic fundamentals and pursuing structural transformation to avoid a debt trap in the future. It is also important for African countries to achieve the following:

- Lower current account deficits;
- Lessen exposure to commodity price volatility through export diversification;
- Design sound investment programmes that contain carefully selected projects and identify key bottlenecks to ensure timely project implementation;
- Combat corruption and misappropriation of funds;
- Ensure greater efficiency in government spending and revenue collection;
- Develop a strategic approach to the identification of the best financing options in terms of financial costs, maturity and payment structures to be matched with new projects.

Ultimately, maintaining debt at sustainable levels is the responsibility of borrowers and lenders. In this regard, more efforts need to be made to encourage United Nations Member States to endorse the principles on promoting responsible sovereign lending and borrowing and reach an agreement on sovereign debt restructuring processes.

3. *Support the revision of a debt sustainability framework that encompasses the achievement of debt sustainability and acknowledges country specificities in its analysis*

In light of the growing development finance requirements of African and developing countries in general, it could be argued that there is a need to revisit current debt sustainability frameworks. Since the 1990s, despite various improvements in the debt sustainability frameworks and analyses, many still consider the framework to be unduly mechanical, backward-looking and restrictive by not differentiating sufficiently between capital and recurrent public spending (UNCTAD, 2004). For many African countries, there remains a tension between accumulating external debt to finance national development strategies and the Sustainable Development Goals, and maintaining external debt sustainability.

Another problem is that there is undue emphasis on broad debt indicators such as debt–GDP or debt–exports, instead of a focus on debt service on domestic and external debt to government revenues. Mainly due to the commodity boom of the early 2000s and recent resource discoveries throughout Africa, many African countries experienced double-digit growth rates in exports. These led to low debt–export ratios, which may not properly reflect their longer term payment capacities, especially in cases where the resources extracted by mostly multinational corporations provided very little revenues to the Government.

Fundamentally, the current debt sustainability framework may be too restrictive on those low-income countries with the capacity to take on more debt that could stimulate growth. There have been concerns among low-income countries in Africa that the Debt Sustainability Framework could lock them into a low-debt low-growth scenario.

There are some options to improve the current Debt Sustainability Framework to allow a limited increase in the debt financing of countries so that African countries can make progress in achieving the Goals without creating a debt overhang. A few elements of this revised framework are as follows:

- Make adjustments in the Framework for investments to finance the Sustainable Development Goals: A revised Framework should have a built-in surveillance system for monitoring the uses of debt, ensuring that countries are borrowing to finance productive investments rather than consumption and are contributing to the achievement of the Goals;

- Place greater emphasis on payment caps on debt service: Refocusing debt sustainability for low-income countries on public debt service payments to government revenues and implementing payment caps on debt service payments for those countries, with a proportional reduction in debt service payments to all creditors, including commercial creditors would be a significant improvement. These debt service limits would need to be part of binding collective action clauses. Given uncertainty regarding whether a debt problem reflects a temporary illiquidity or a more permanent debt overhang situation, debt service caps could be implemented on a temporary basis without reducing total debt stocks. If it becomes clear that a country faces a longer term debt overhang, a debt stock reduction would need to be implemented.

4. *Foster domestic financial deepening to enhance domestic resources and attract diaspora savings*

The report has noted that Africa has made important progress in domestic financial sector development and financial deepening. It is encouraging that countries have been able to issue bonds and various other more marketable and long-term instruments. Furthermore, African countries have adopted policies aimed at developing their domestic debt markets, with the active support of official international financial institutions such as the African Development Bank, IMF, OECD and the World Bank.

These are encouraging trends, but there is scope for further deepening. For example, the potential of the savings generated by the retirement benefit industry and the insurance sector should be further exploited. Also, facilitating and lowering the cost of formal remittance channels will allow the attraction of more remittances through these channels. Financial deepening will also make it possible to mobilize and use diaspora savings, for example through diaspora bonds, foreign-currency-denominated deposits and syndicated loans with remittances as collateral.

The rise in domestic debt as a component of domestic resource mobilization for development finance could help reduce Africa's dependence on the volatility of foreign direct investment and official development assistance, and increase Africa's policy space. This may also strengthen policy accountability and country ownership of development strategies, given that a greater reliance on domestic sources of development finance can reduce external debt vulnerabilities.

5. *Harness the potential of public–private partnerships by strengthening public–private partnership policy frameworks at the national and regional levels while keeping debt sustainability in check*

Governments should have adequate legal and policy frameworks to optimize the use of public–private partnerships for their development while minimizing the pitfalls of public–private partnership failure. In this regard, regulation and policymaking have yet to play a major role in establishing how such partnerships are to be treated, in terms of sustainable debt management and general economic development. Developing regulation that guides an appropriate valuation and recording of public–private partnerships should be accompanied by defined risk management principles and the consideration of a contingent liabilities fund to address failing public–private partnerships when these merit government intervention.

For better public–private partnership management, African countries could consider the use of the Debt Sustainability Framework template to design customized scenarios in both external and public debt sustainability analyses. One such scenario is a standardized stress test that resembles a generic contingent liability shock. Where information is available, a more country-specific scenario may be warranted to capture contingent liabilities arising from, inter alia, State-owned enterprises, subnational governments, public–private partnerships and weaknesses in the financial sector.

It is equally important for African Governments to be vigilant of the risk associated with contingent liabilities. Debt managers should ensure that the impact of risks associated with contingent liabilities on the Government's financial position, including its overall liquidity, is taken into consideration when designing debt management strategies. Although clearly negotiations and arrangements between a Government (particularly in the case of State-owned enterprises) and private companies are bound to confidentiality, nonetheless information on general financial terms and conditions should be made public. If the Government proves insolvent, these liabilities may become a public concern. This also requires scope for strengthening parliamentary scrutiny, with members of parliament responsible for approving arrangements on an ad hoc basis and not the entire envelope for new borrowing for the year. If approval on a loan-by-loan basis creates a bottleneck, scrutiny may be required for contracts above a certain threshold. Strengthening institutional capacities for rating, monitoring and managing debt, whether public or private, is critical for African countries, as this will help them manage their debt levels in a more sustainable manner. UNCTAD can assist African countries in developing statistical series and capacity in the areas of domestic debt, external private debt, debt composition and sovereign debt restructuring.

6. *Enhance international and regional cooperation and build institutional capacity in addressing Africa's financing needs*

Regional integration could play a critical role in coordinating and mainstreaming key regulatory and institutional dimensions of broader financing for development initiatives in the context of Agenda 2063 and the 2030 Agenda for Sustainable

Development. The African Union and the New Partnership for Africa's Development should be supported in reinvigorating efforts to bolster national and regional strategies, build the necessary institutional frameworks and promote resource mobilization instruments such as regional stock exchanges, the African Credit Guarantee Facility and the Programme for Infrastructure Development in Africa. This will require significant political and effective pooling of continental resources.

Across all the financing flows, there is still scope to improve debt management; coordination within the African Union, coupled with a whole-of-government approach, could help strengthen medium-term debt management strategies. The promotion of the UNCTAD principles on responsible sovereign lending and borrowing could be particularly important in this regard. Africa will need to continue striving towards stronger debt management capacity. Several training programmes to strengthen debt-management capacity have been promoted in recent years, but this new complexity of financing options requires a new skill set towards private financial markets that government officials may not have developed yet. At the international level, cooperation in tax matters and illicit financial flows should be sustained and enhanced. Africa cannot combat illicit financial flows on its own; it would greatly benefit from multilateral support in building its institutional capacities to deal with such flows and international commitment to tackling this important issue. Capacities of public revenue authorities should therefore be strengthened in various areas, particularly with regard to tax issues and detailing and curtailing illicit financial flows.

7. Overcome data limitations and build analytical capacities for debt monitoring and management

There are still considerable problems related to data availability. After many initiatives, especially related to debt management in African countries, it is surprising how little data on domestic debt and government revenues are publicly available. While IMF and the World Bank possess such data for most countries, especially with respect to heavily indebted poor countries in Africa, which they monitor on a regular basis, most of this data are not readily available to the public. For example, the World Development Indicators and Global Development Finance databases contain no data on domestic debt and have considerable gaps with regard to government revenues. The unavailability of such data contributes to the use of less useful debt indicators such as debt–GDP and debt–export ratios. Improved institutional capacities for the collection, collation and analysis of debt data will be central to improved debt sustainability, particularly where developing countries are concerned. The Debt Management and Financial Analysis System of UNCTAD is a good illustration of how technical cooperation can support this process in Africa. It has developed a specialized debt management and financial analysis software to meet the operational, statistical and analytical needs of debt managers. This may help developing countries improve the quality of their debt database, contributing to better transparency and accountability, debt reporting and debt sustainability analysis.

NOTES
AND
REFERENCES

NOTES

1   Yield is the income return on an investment and refers to the interest or dividends received from a security, usually expressed annually as a percentage based on the investment's cost or its current market or face value. Return is the actual earnings of an investor on an investment during a certain time period in the past and includes interest, dividends and capital gains (such as an increase in the share price). Return is retrospective, describing the concrete earnings of an investment. Yield, however, is prospective, as it measures the income, such as interest and dividends, that an investment may earn and excludes capital gains.

2   As of 1 July 2015, low-income economies are defined as those with a GNI per capita, calculated using the World Bank atlas method, of $1,045 or less in 2014, middle-income economies are those with a GNI per capita of more than $1,045 but less than $12,736 and high-income economies are those with a GNI per capita of $12,736 or more. Lower middle-income and upper middle-income economies are divided at GNI per capita of $4,125 (World Bank, 2016d).

3   The emphasis of the Addis Ababa Action Agenda on domestic resource mobilization and on private sector roles has been criticized in some circles (Deen, 2015).

4   Domestic resource mobilization accompanied by a reversal of illicit financial flows has recently gained ground as being central to Africa's options for financing its development needs, as encapsulated in the Sustainable Development Goals and Agenda 2063. Illicit financial flows have been estimated to cost Africa about $50 billion per year (African Union and United Nations Economic Commission for Africa Conference of Ministers of Finance, Planning and Economic Development, 2014).

5   Some studies state that stock markets do not play a particularly useful role in either early or later catch-up development (Singh, 2010).

6   Generally, the relative share of external debt owed by private debtors in Africa is low. Although ratios of private external debt to GNI are rising, they are far lower than those prevalent in Asia and Latin America and the Caribbean (UNCTAD, 2015b).

7   This section focuses on external debt to GNI ratios as these are the most commonly understood and used reference points in many discussions on indebtedness. However, UNCTAD has also computed net present value estimates of total external debt, given that there are changes in discount rates over time and often large differences in loan periods and interest rates across countries. In 2006–2013, the net present value of external debt in Africa rose in non-heavily indebted poor countries yet the ratio of net present value debt to GNI was stable, at around 20 per cent, for both heavily indebted poor countries and non-heavily indebted poor countries. Most trends were similar to those presented in table 2.

8   In January 2014–December 2015, crude petroleum prices declined by 47 per cent, minerals, ores and metals by 22 per cent, vegetable oilseeds and oils by 20 per cent and food and tropical beverages and agricultural raw materials by 14 per cent each (UNCTAD, 2016). Both oil and non-oil exporters have thus been affected by a decline in commodity prices, although the sharpest contraction is in oil.

9   As at November 2015, data from the World Bank (2016b) were not available for Djibouti, Equatorial Guinea, Libya, Namibia, Somalia or South Sudan. As of December 2015, Seychelles is no longer covered in this database.

10 The World Bank defined middle-income status in 2013 as current GNI per capita exceeding $1,035. By this measure, in 2006 there were 15 middle-income countries in Africa (Algeria, Botswana, Cabo Verde, the Congo, Egypt, Equatorial Guinea, Gabon, Libya, Mauritius, Morocco, Namibia, Seychelles, South Africa, Swaziland and Tunisia) and in 2013 there were 25 middle-income countries (now including Cameroon, Côte d'Ivoire, Ghana, Kenya, Lesotho, Mauritania, Nigeria, Sao Tome and Principe, the Sudan and Zambia).

11 As of December 2015, Seychelles is no longer covered in the World Bank, 2016b.

12 Davies et al. (forthcoming) note that Uganda does not access international financial markets because of the expense of sovereign bonds and concerns that public debt could rise to unsustainable levels during a currency depreciation, increasing bond yields.

13 The yield curve shows several yields or interest rates across different contract terms (such as 2-month, 2-year and 20-year terms) for a similar debt contract, depicting the relation between the (level of the) interest rate (or cost of borrowing) and time to maturity, known as the term of the debt, for a given borrower in a given currency.

14 Rollover is the extension or transfer of a debt or other financial arrangement. Rollover risk is a risk associated with the refinancing of debt. If interest rates rise adversely, countries must refinance their debts at a higher rate and incur greater interest charges in the future.

15 The grace period is the period from the date of signature of a loan or issuance of a financial instrument to the date of first repayment of the principal. Maturity refers to the number of years to original maturity date, which is the sum of the grace and repayment periods. The repayment period is the period from the first to the last repayment of the principal.

16 The factors analysed include GDP growth, international reserves over GDP, trade openness, undervaluation of exchange rate, growth rate of private credit, fiscal and current account balance, inflation and control of corruption.

17 Low-income economies are defined as in note 2. The United Nations least developed countries category is defined by a different set of criteria. In 2016, of 31 low-income countries listed by the World Bank, 29 were least developed countries and 26 were in Africa.

18 The country policy and institutional assessment index is compiled annually by the World Bank for all countries eligible for support under the International Development Association, including blend countries, ranging from 1 (lowest) to 6 (highest). The index consists of 16 indicators grouped into the following four categories: economic management; structural policies; policies for social inclusion and equity; and public sector management and institutions. The Framework uses the index to classify countries into one of three policy performance categories according to the strengths of their policies and institutions; countries with a score equal to or less than 3.25

are considered to have weak policies and institutions, countries with a score greater than 3.25 and less than 3.75 are considered to have medium level policies and institutions and countries with a score equal to or greater than 3.75 are considered to have strong policies and institutions (IMF, 2013b).

19 A collective action clause allows a supermajority of bond holders to agree to debt restructuring that is legally binding on all holders of a bond, including those who vote against the restructuring. Such clauses are a means of enabling easier coordination among bond holders.

20 Such risks are currently analysed as a generic shock of an increase of 10 per cent of GDP in debt, creating flows in the second year of a projection period and country-specific customized scenarios if information is available (IMF, 2013b).

21 Under the terms of the 2002 exception access policy, the only option for IMF would have been to condition support to the implementation of a debt restructuring operation that was of sufficient depth to enable IMF to conclude that, post restructuring, the member's indebtedness would be sustainable with a high probability. Out of concern that an upfront debt restructuring operation would have potentially systemic effects, IMF amended the framework in 2010 to allow the requirement to determine debt sustainability with high probability to be waived in circumstances where there is a high risk of international systemic spillovers.

22 Assistance through the catastrophe containment and relief trust is currently available to low-income countries eligible for concessional borrowing through the poverty reduction and growth trust that also have either a per capita income below the International Development Association operational cut-off (currently $1,215) or, for States with a population below 1.5 million, a per capita income below twice the cut-off (currently $2,430).

23 In some African countries, State and municipal authorities have the capacity to borrow (often by issuing State, municipal or city infrastructure bonds) beyond the control of federal or central Government authorities, which may pose future debt sustainability problems.

24 The term original sin in an economics context was originally used by Eichengreen and Hausmann (2003) and refers to the difficulty faced by countries in borrowing in local currency and with long maturities in the domestic debt market.

25 This may also reflect the existence of uncovered interest rate parity effects, whereby the parity condition in which exposure to foreign exchange risk (unanticipated changes in exchange rates) is uninhibited. Thus, the gap between domestic and external interest rates could be plausibly explained by inflation differentials and expected foreign exchange movements.

26 In the case of Zambia, a vulture fund, having bought a debt for $3 million, sued Zambia for $55 million and was awarded $15.5 million. Vulture funds exert pressure on a sovereign debtor by attempting to obtain attachment of its assets abroad.

27 The World Bank database records contractual arrangements with and without investments between a Government and private parties. The information provided includes project counts and investments of public–private partnerships. Investments can be transformed into physical assets, which are resources the project company

commits to for investment in facilities during the contract period. Investments can be made in new facilities or in the expansion and modernization of existing ones, or in the form of payments to the Government, which are resources the project company spends on acquiring government assets, such as State-owned enterprises, rights to provide services in a specific area or the use of specific radio spectrums.

28 The World Bank Private Participation in Infrastructure database does not register information on Libya and Equatorial Guinea.

29 Public–private partnerships in the World Bank Private Participation in Infrastructure database are divided into four main sectors: energy, telecommunications, transport, and water and sewerage. The telecommunications sector exclusively focuses on telecommunications in fixed, mobile and/or long-distance access. The energy sector encompasses public–private partnerships for the electricity and natural gas subsectors, while the transport category comprises airports, seaports, railways and toll roads. Water and sewerage includes treatment plants as well as utilities.

30 Greenfield projects are projects developed through capital investments from the ground up. They generally imply that a new operational facility or infrastructure is built or expanded, representing a physical asset that was non-existent prior the investment.

31 Full divestiture is sometimes perceived as privatization, as it occurs when the full interests of a Government in a utility asset or State-owned enterprise are transferred to the private sector. A fully divested or privatized utility or public service is distinguishable from a private commercial enterprise in that the Government generally retains some indirect form of control or mechanism for regulation over the privatized utility, in the form of a licence granted to the entity to deliver the service to the public.

32 Foster and Briceño-Garmendia (2010) in a comprehensive assessment of capital expenditure on infrastructure in sub-Saharan Africa find that the private and public sectors account for $9.4 billion per year each. However, there is no further disaggregation of the data available to determine the share of public–private partnerships in this total. If operations and maintenance costs are added to capital expenditure, then two thirds of infrastructure spending is covered by the private sector each year.

33 All African countries are members of at least one regional economic community, and most are members of two, and are thus actively engaged in regional integration processes.

34 See www.privatesector.ecowas.int/en/III/Supplementary_ Act_Investment.pdf, accessed 18 April 2016.

35 See www.sadc.int/files/4213/5332/6872/Protocol_on_Finance__Investment2006.pdf, accessed 18 April 2016.

36 However, the debt sustainability framework template allows users to design customized scenarios in both the external and public debt sustainability analyses. One such scenario is a standardized stress test that resembles a generic contingent liability shock – an increase of 10 per cent of GDP in debt – creating flows in the second year of a projection period. Where information is available, a more country-

specific scenario may be warranted to capture contingent liabilities arising from, inter alia, State-owned enterprises, subnational governments, public–private partnerships and weaknesses in the financial sector.

37 Distressed projects are those where the Government or the operator has either requested contract termination or those that are in international arbitration.

38 There have been some documented cases of public–private partnership failure in Africa. See Jubilee Debt Campaign Report, 2015.

39 A syndicated loan is a loan by a group of lenders (a syndicate) working together to provide funds for a single borrower.

40 See www.gfmd.org/pfp/ppd/1861, accessed 14 April 2016.

41 The Stolen Asset Recovery Initiative, launched in 2007 by the United Nations Office on Drugs and Crime and the World Bank, provides technical assistance in tracing stolen wealth, asset seizure and confiscation, and enlisting international cooperation (Brun et al., 2011).

42 Defined as loans with an original grant element of 25 per cent or more.

REFERENCES

Abbas SMA and Christensen JE (2007). The Role of domestic debt markets in economic growth: An empirical Investigation for low-income countries and emerging markets. IMF Working Paper No. 07/127.

Adams P (2015). Africa debt rising. Africa Research Institute. 22 January. Available at africaresearchinstitute.org/publications/africa-debt-rising-2/ (accessed 18 March 2015).

Adelegan OJ and Radzewicz-Bak B (2009). What determines bond market development in sub-Saharan Africa? IMF Working Paper No. 09/213.

African Capacity-Building Foundation (2015). *Africa Capacity Report 2015 – Capacity Imperatives for Domestic Resource Mobilization in Africa*. Harare.

African Development Bank, OECD, United Nations Development Programme and United Nations Economic Commission for Africa (2012). *African Economic Outlook 2012: Promoting Youth Employment*. OECD Publishing, Paris.

African Union (2001). New Partnership for Africa's Development. Abuja.

African Union (2015). *Agenda 2063: The Africa We Want*, third edition, popular version. Addis Ababa.

African Union, African Development Bank and New Partnership for Africa's Development (2010). Programme for Infrastructure Development in Africa – Interconnecting, integrating and transforming a continent. Available at nepad.org/sites/default/files/PIDA%20Executive%20Summary%20-%20English.pdf (accessed 13 April 2016).

African Union and United Nations Economic Commission for Africa Conference of Ministers of Finance, Planning and Economic Development (2014). Track it! Stop it! Get it! Illicit financial flows. Report of the High-Level Panel on Illicit Financial Flows from Africa. Available at uneca.org/sites/default/files/PublicationFiles/iff_main_report_26feb_en.pdf (accessed 13 April 2016).

Akyüz Y (2014). Internationalization of finance and changing vulnerabilities in emerging and developing economies. UNCTAD Discussion Paper No. 217.

Bank of Ghana (2015). *Annual Reports*, 2004–2014. Available at bog.gov.gh/index.php?option=com_content&view=article&id=113&Itemid=172 (accessed 13 April 2016).

Bank of Zambia (2015). *Annual Reports,* 2004–2014. Available at boz.zm/%28S%280ea5pb45vfolnqizj4k3xx45%29%29/GeneralContent.aspx?site=39 (accessed 13 April 2016).

Battaile B, Hernandez FL and Norambuena V (2015). Debt sustainability in sub-Saharan Africa: Unravelling country-specific risks. Policy Research Working Paper No. 7523. World Bank.

Brun J-P, Gray L, Scott C and Stephenson KM (2011). *Asset Recovery Handbook: A Guide for Practitioners*. World Bank, Washington, D.C.

Caliari A (2014). Post-2015 infrastructure finance: The new debt threat? Available at developmentprogress.org/blog/2014/02/10/post-2015-infrastructure-finance-new-debt-threat (accessed 18 April 2016).

Canavire-Bacarreza GJ, Neumayer E and Nunnenkamp P (2015). Why aid is unpredictable: An empirical analysis of the gap between actual and planned aid flows. *Journal of International Development*. 27(4):440–463.

Central Bank of Kenya (2015). *Annual Reports*, 2000–2015. Available at centralbank. go.ke/index.php/cbk-annual-reports (accessed 13 April 2016).

Central Bank of Nigeria (2015). *Central Bank and Debt Management Office Annual Reports*, 2000–2014. Available at cenbank.org/documents/annualreports.asp (accessed 18 April 2016).

Chinzana Z, Kedir A and Sandjong D (2015). Growth and development finance required for achieving Sustainable Development Goals in Africa. Presented at the African Economic Conference. Kinshasa. 2–4 November. Available at afdb.org/uploads/tx_llafdbpapers/ Growth_and_Development_Finance_Required_for_Achieving_Sustainable_ Development_Goals__SDGs__in_Africa.pdf (accessed 13 April 2016).

Christensen J (2004). Domestic debt markets in sub-Saharan Africa. IMF Working Paper No. 04/46.

Davies F, Long C and Wabwire M (forthcoming). Age of choice: Uganda in the new development finance landscape. Overseas Development Institute Working Paper.

Deen T (2015). Civil society sceptical over action agenda to finance development. Inter Press Service. 15 July. Available at ipsnews.net/2015/07/civil-society-sceptical-over-action-agenda-to-finance-development/ (accessed 23 March 2016).

Economic Community of West African States: privatesector.ecowas.int/en/III/ Supplementary_Act_Investment.pdf (accessed 18 April 2016).

Economic Justice Network (2011). Walking the talk on illicit financial flows: The G20's responsibility in combating illicit capital flight. Available at taxjusticeafrica.net/ wp-content/uploads/2015/11/Policy-Brief-Illicit-Flows-Tax-Evasion-SA-G20.pdf (accessed 18 April 2016).

Eichengreen B and Hausmann R (2003). Original sin: The road to redemption. Available at eml.berkeley.edu/~eichengr/research/osroadaug21-03.pdf (accessed 13 April 2016).

Farlam P (2005). Working together: Assessing public–private partnerships in Africa. Policy Focus Series. South African Institute of International Affairs. Available at oecd. org/investment/investmentfordevelopment/34867724.pdf (accessed 13 April 2016).

Ferrarini B (2008). Proposal for a contingency debt sustainability framework. *World Development*. 36(12):2547–2565.

Financial Times (2016). Emerging market debt: A trawl for yield. 17 March.

Flassbeck H and Panizza U (2008). Debt sustainability and debt composition. Presented at the Workshop on Debt, Finance and Emerging Issues in Financial Integration. New York. 8–9 April. Available at un.org/esa/ ffd/events/2008debtworkshop/papers/Flassbeck-Panizza-Paper.pdf (accessed 13 April 2016).

Foster V and Briceño-Garmendia C, eds. (2010). *Africa's Infrastructure: A Time for Transformation*. World Bank and Africa Development Forum. Washington, D.C.

Lewis, JD (2013). What comes after debt relief? Some preliminary thoughts. Great Insights. 2(1):8–9.

Ghana Ministry of Finance (2015). Annual fiscal report data. Available at mofep.gov.gh/.

Greenhill R and Ali A (2013). Paying for progress: How will emerging post-2015 goals be financed in the new aid landscape? Overseas Development Institute Working Paper No. 366.

Griffiths J, Martin M, Pereira J and Strawson T (2014). Financing for development post-2015: Improving the contribution of private finance. European Parliament Directorate-General for External Policies of the Union. Available at europa.eu/eyd2015/sites/default/files/users/maja.ljubic/expo-deve_ et2014433848_en.pdf (accessed 13 April 2016).

Gunter B (forthcoming). Financing Africa's development: Priorities, options and challenges. UNCTAD Discussion Paper.

Gutman J, Sy A and Chattopadhyay S (2015). *Financing African Infrastructure: Can the World Deliver?* Brookings Institution, Washington, D.C.

Guzman, M and Heymann, D (2015). The IMF debt sustainability analysis: Issues and problems. *Journal of Globalization and Development*. 6(2):387–404.

Herkenrath M (2014). Illicit financial flows and their developmental impacts: An overview. *International Development Policy*. Available at poldev.revues.org/1863#text (accessed 18 April 2016).

Hill C and MacPherson MF, eds. (2004). *Promoting and Sustaining Economic Reform in Zambia*. Harvard University Press. Cambridge, Massachusetts.

Howse R (2007). The concept of odious debt in public international law. UNCTAD Discussion Paper No. 185.

IMF (2005). World Economic Outlook April 2005 – *Globalization and External Imbalances*. Washington, D.C.

_____ (2007). *Evaluation Report: The IMF and Aid to Sub-Saharan Africa*. Washington, D.C.

_____(2013a). Regional Economic Outlook: Sub-Saharan Africa – *Building Momentum in a Multi-Speed World*. Washington, D.C.

_____(2013b). Staff guidance note on the application of the joint Bank-Fund debt sustainability framework for low-income countries. Available at imf.org/external/np/pp/eng/2013/110513.pdf (accessed 25 March 2016).

_____(2014a). *Regional Economic Outlook: Sub-Saharan Africa – Staying the Course*. Washington, D.C.

_____(2014b). The Fund's lending framework and sovereign debt – preliminary considerations. Available at imf.org/external/np/pp/eng/2014/052214a.pdf (accessed 13 April 2016).

_____(2015a). *Regional Economic Outlook: Sub-Saharan Africa – Navigating Headwinds*. Washington, D.C.

_____(2015b) Zambia: Debt Sustainability Analysis – Staff report for the 2015 Article IV Consultation. IMF Country Report No. 15/152. Washington, D.C. Available at imf.org/external/pubs/cat/longres.aspx?sk=42999.0 (accessed 20 April 2016).

IMF and World Bank (2012). Revisiting the Debt Sustainability Framework for Low-Income Countries. Available at imf.org/external/np/pp/eng/2012/011212.pdf (accessed 20 April 2016).

IMF, World Bank, European Bank for Reconstruction and Development and OECD (2013). Local currency bond markets – a diagnostic framework. Available at imf.org/external/np/pp/eng/2013/070913.pdf (accessed 13 April 2016).

International Energy Agency (2012). *World Energy Outlook 2012*. Paris.

Jubilee Debt Campaign (2012). State of debt: Putting an end to 30 years of crisis. Available at jubileedebt.org.uk/reports-briefings/... (accessed 13 April 2016).

_____(2015). The new debt trap: How the response to the last global financial crisis has laid the ground for the next. Available at jubileedebt.org.uk/reports-briefings/report/the-new-debt-trap (accessed 13 April 2016).

Kar D and Cartwright-Smith D (2010). Illicit financial flows from Africa: Hidden resource for development in Report of the High-Level Panel on. Available at gfintegrity.org/storage/gfip/documents/reports/gfi_africareport_web.pdf (accessed 13 April 2016).

Kar D and Freitas S (2011). Illicit financial flows from developing countries over the decade ending 2009. Available at gfintegrity.org/wp-content/uploads/2014/05/HIGHRES-Illicit_Financial_Flows_from_Developing_Countries_over_the_Decade_Ending_2009.pdf (accessed 13 April 2016).

Kauf A (2015). Financing as key enabling factor. Presented at the Multi-Year Expert Meeting on Transport, Trade Logistics and Trade Facilitation. Geneva. May. Available at unctad.org/meetings/en/Presentation/Ansgar%20KAUF.pdf (accessed 13 April 2016).

Kenya National Treasury (2014). *Annual Public Debt Report July 2013–June 2014*. Available at treasury.go.ke/(accessed 13 April 2016).

Ketkar SL and Ratha D, eds. (2009). Future-flow securitization. In: Innovative Financing for Development. World Bank. Washington, D.C.

_____ (2010). Diaspora bonds: Tapping the diaspora during difficult times. *Journal of International Commerce, Economics and Policy*. 1(2):251.

Kremer M and Jayachandran S (2002). Odious debt. National Bureau of Economic Research Working Paper Series. Working Paper No. 8953.

Maana I (2008). Compilation and analysis of data on securitized public debt in Kenya. In: Irving Fisher Committee on Central Bank Statistics Bulletin No. 31. Measuring Financial Innovation and Its Impact: Proceedings of the Irving Fisher Committee Conference. Bank for International Settlements. Basel: 35–43.

Maimbo SM and Ratha D, eds. (2005). *Remittances: Development Impact and Future Prospects*. World Bank, Washington, D.C.

Martin M (2015). Forestalling risks from contingent liabilities. Presented at the Tenth International Debt Management Conference. Geneva, 23–25 November. Available at unctad.org/en/pages/MeetingDetails.aspx?meetingid=702 (accessed 13 April 2016).

Mavrotas G, ed. (2008). *Domestic Resource Mobilization and Financial Development.* Palgrave Macmillan in association with the United Nations University – World Institute for Development Economics Research. New York.

Ndikumana L and Boyce K (2008). New estimates of capital flight from sub-Saharan African countries: Linkages with external borrowing and policy options. Working Paper No. 166. Political Economy Research Institute. University of Massachusetts.

_____(2011). Africa's Odious Debts: *How Foreign Loans and Capital Flight Bled a Continent.* Zed Books. London and New York.

OECD (2015a). *African Central Government Debt – Statistical Yearbook 2003–2013.* OECD Publishing, Paris.

_____(2015b). Development Cooperation Report 2015: Making Partnerships Effective Coalitions for Action. OECD Publishing, Paris.

Orozco M and Fedewa R (2006). Leveraging efforts on remittances and financial intermediation. Institute for the Integration of Latin America and the Caribbean Working Paper No. 24.

Panizza U (2008). Domestic and external public debt in developing countries. UNCTAD Discussion Paper No. 188.

Pigato MA and Tang W (2015). China and Africa: Expanding economic ties in an evolving global context. Working Paper No. 95161. World Bank.

Prizzon A and Mustapha S (2014). Debt sustainability in heavily indebted poor countries in a new age of choice: Taking stock of the debt relief initiatives and implications of the new development finance landscape for public debt sustainability. Overseas Development Institute Working Paper No. 397.

Pulitzer Centre on Crisis Reporting (2014). Zambia: The end of vulture funds? Available at unctad.org/en/pages/MeetingDetails.aspx?meetingid=702 (accessed 13 April 2016).

Qizilbash A (2011). Public–private partnerships and the value of the process: The case of sub-Saharan Africa. *International Public Management Review.* 12(2).

Ratha D (2013). The impact of remittances on economic growth and poverty reduction. Migration Policy Institute Policy Briefs.

Ratha D and Plaza S (2011). Harnessing diasporas: Africa can tap some of its millions of emigrants to help development efforts. Available at imf.org/external/pubs/ft/fandd/2011/09/pdf/ratha.pdf (accessed 13 April 2016).

Romero MJ (2015). What lies beneath? A critical assessment of PPPs [public–private partnerships] and their impact on sustainable development. European Network on Debt and Development.

Schmidt-Traub G (2015). Investment needs to achieve the Sustainable Development Goals – understanding the billions and trillions. Sustainable Development Solutions Network Working Paper, version 2.

Shaoul J (2009). Using the private sector to finance capital expenditure: The financial realities. In: Akintoye A and Beck M, eds. Policy, *Finance and Management for Public–Private Partnership.* Blackwell Publishing Ltd. Oxford.

Singh A (2010). Are the institutions of the stock market and the market for corporate control evolutionary advances for developing countries? Munich Personal Research Papers in Economics Archive No. 24346.

Southern African Development Community. Protocol on Finance and Investment. Available at sadc.int/files/4213/5332/6872/Protocol_on_Finance__Investment2006. pdf (accessed 18 April 2016).

South Africa National Treasury (2015). *National Debt Report 2014–2015*. Available at treasury.gov.za/publications/other/Debt%20Management%20Report%202014-15. pdf (accessed 13 April 2016).

Spanjers J and Frede Foss H (2015). Illicit financial flows and development indices. Available at gfintegrity.org/wp-content/uploads/2015/05/Illicit-Financial-Flows-and-Development-Indices-2008-2012.pdf (accessed 13 April 2016).

Standard and Poor's (2014). Ghana downgraded to B- on external risks. Available at standardandpoors.com/en_US/web/guest/article/-/view/type/HTML/id/1365808 (accessed 6 March 2016).

Sy A (2013). Financing Africa: Moving beyond foreign aid to issuing Eurobonds. Brookings Institution. 13 September. Available at brookings.edu/research/opinions/2013/09/13-financing-africa-foreign-aid-eurobonds-sy (accessed 13 April 2016).

Tafirenyika M (2015). How healthy is Africa's sovereign bond debt? Analysts caution against accumulating too much. United Nations Department of Public Information Africa Renewal 29(1):5–6.

Task Force on Development Impact of Illicit Financial Flows (2011). Final Report. Available at leadinggroup.org/IMG/pdf_Final_report_Task_Force_EN.pdf (accessed 13 April 2016).

Tyson JE (2015). *Sub-Saharan Africa International Sovereign Bonds, Part II: Risks for Issuers*. Overseas Development Institute, London.

UNCTAD (2004). *Economic Development in Africa: Debt Sustainability: Oasis or Mirage?* United Nations publication. Sales No. E.04.II.D.37. New York and Geneva.

_____(2009). *Enhancing the Role of Domestic Financial Resources in Africa's Development – A Policy Handbook*. United Nations publication. New York and Geneva.

_____(2012a). Draft principles on promoting responsible sovereign lending and borrowing. Available at http://unctad.org/en/Pages/GDS/Sovereign-Debt-Portal/Sovereign-Lending-and-Borrowing.aspx (accessed 13 April 2016).

_____(2012b). *The Least Developed Countries Report 2012: Harnessing Remittances and Diaspora Knowledge to Build Productive Capacities*. United Nations publication. Sales No. E.12.II.D.18. New York and Geneva.

_____(2014). *World Investment Report 2014: Investing in the Sustainable Development Goals – An Action Plan*. United Nations publication. Sales No. E.14. II.D.1. New York and Geneva.

_____(2015a). *The Least Developed Countries Report 2015: Transforming Rural Economies*. United Nations publication. Sales No. E.15.II.D.7. New York and Geneva.

_____(2015b). *Trade and Development Report, 2015: Making the International Financial Architecture Work for Development*. United Nations publication. Sales No. E.15.II.D.4. New York and Geneva.

_____(2015c). *Economic Development in Africa Report 2015: Unlocking the Potential of Africa's Services Trade for Growth and Development*. United Nations publication. Sales No. E.15.II.D.2. New York and Geneva.

_____(2015d). *World Investment Report 2015: Reforming International Investment Governance*. United Nations publication. Sales No. E.15.II.D.5. New York and Geneva.

_____(2015e). *From Decisions to Actions: Report of the Secretary-General of UNCTAD to UNCTAD XIV*. United Nations publication. New York and Geneva.

_____(2016). UNCTADStat database. Available at unctadstat.unctad.org/ ReportFolders/reportFolders.aspx (accessed 19 April 2016).

United Nations (2005). In larger freedom: Towards development, security and human rights for all. Report of the Secretary-General. A/59/2005. New York. 21 March.

United Nations Economic Commission for Africa (2015). *Africa Regional Report on the Sustainable Development Goals*. Addis Ababa.

United Nations Economic Commission for Africa and New Partnership for Africa's Development (2014). *Mobilizing Domestic Financial Resources for Implementing New Partnership for Africa's Development National and Regional Programmes and Projects – Africa Looks Within*. Johannesburg, South Africa.

United Nations Economic Commission for Latin America and the Caribbean (2011). The economic infrastructure gap in Latin America and the Caribbean. Facilitation of Transport and Trade in Latin America Bulletin. 293 (1) Santiago. Available at repositorio.cepal.org/bitstream/handle/11362/36339/FAL-293-WEB-ENG-2_ en.pdf?sequence=1 (accessed 20 April 2016).

United Republic of Tanzania (2002). National Debt Strategy: Domestic and total debt. Available at mof.go.tz/mofdocs/debt/nationaldebtstrategy.pdf (accessed 13 April 2016).

Bank of the United Republic of Tanzania (2015). *Annual Reports, 2000–2014*. Available at bottz.org/publications/ FinancialReports/FinancialStatements/2014/BOT%20 annual%20report%202014.pdf (accessed 13 April 2016).

Vaggi G and Prizzon A (2014). On the sustainability of external debt: is debt relief enough? Cambridge Journal of Economics. 38(5):1155–1169.

te Velde DW (2014). Sovereign bonds in sub-Saharan Africa: Good for growth or ahead of time? Overseas Development Institute Briefing No. 87.

Were M (2001). The impact of external debt on economic growth in Kenya: An empirical assessment. United Nations University World Institute for Development Economics Research Discussion Paper No. 2001/116.

World Bank (2012). *Transformation Through Infrastructure.* Washington, D.C.

_____(2014). *Building Integrated Markets within the East African Community – East African Community Opportunities in Public-Private Partnership Approaches to the Region's Infrastructure Needs.* Washington, D.C.

_____(2015a). *International Debt Statistics 2015.* Washington, D.C.

_____(2015b). Public Private Infrastructure Advisory Facility Private Participation in Infrastructure database. Available at ppi.worldbank.org/ (accessed 20 April 2016).

_____(2015c). Migration and remittances: Recent developments and outlook. Migration and Development Brief 24. Available at siteresources.worldbank.org/ INTPROSPECTS/Resources/334934-1288990760745/Migration and Development Brief24.pdf (accessed 13 April 2016).

_____(2016a). *Global Economic Prospects – Spillovers amid Weak Growth.* Washington, D.C.

_____(2016b). International Debt Statistics database. Available at data.worldbank. org/data-catalog/international-debt-statistics.

_____(2016c). World Development Indicators database. Available at data. worldbank.org/data-catalog/world-development-indicators.

_____(2016d). Country and lending groups. Available at data.worldbank.org/ about/country-and-lending-groups (accessed 8 March 2016).

_____(2016e). Public–private partnerships. Available at worldbank.org/en/topic/ publicprivatepartnerships/overview#2 (accessed 20 April 2016).

World Bank and Debt Management Facility (2013). Africa since debt relief: Considerations for the Debt Sustainability Framework. Available at siteresources.worldbank.org/ INTDEBTDEPT/Resources/468980-1170954447788/3430000-1358445852781/ KB_AfricanHIPCs.pdf (accessed 13 April 2016).

World Bank and IMF (2014). Factsheet: The Joint World Bank–IMF Debt Sustainability Framework for Low-Income Countries. Available at imf.org/external/np/exr/facts/ jdsf.htm (accessed 13 April 2016).

World Bank and IMF (2015). Public debt vulnerabilities in low-income countries: The evolving landscape. Board Report No. 101021. Available at documents.worldbank. org/curated/en/2015/12/25472395/public-debt-vulnerabilities-low-income-countries-evolving-landscape (accessed 13 April 2016)

Economic Development in Africa – Report Series:

2000   Capital Flows and Growth in Africa – TD/B/47/4 – UNCTAD/GDS/MDPB/7
Contributors: Yilmaz Akyüz, Kamran Kousari (team leader), Korkut Boratav
(consultant).

2001   Performance, Prospects and Policy Issues – UNCTAD/GDS/AFRICA/1
Contributors: Yilmaz Akyüz, Kamran Kousari (team leader), Korkut Boratav
(consultant).

2002   From Adjustment to Poverty Reduction: What is New? – UNCTAD/GDS/
AFRICA/2
Contributors: Yilmaz Akyüz, Kamran Kousari (team leader), Korkut Boratav
(consultant).

2003   Trade Performance and Commodity Dependence – UNCTAD/GDS/
AFRICA/2003/1
Contributors: Yilmaz Akyüz, Kamran Kousari (team leader), Samuel Gayi.

2004   Debt Sustainability: Oasis or Mirage? – UNCTAD/GDS/AFRICA/2004/1
Contributors: Kamran Kousari (team leader), Samuel Gayi, Bernhard
Gunter (consultant), Phillip Cobbina (research).

2005   Rethinking the Role of Foreign Direct Investment – UNCTAD/GDS/
AFRICA/2005/1
Contributors: Kamran Kousari (team leader), Samuel Gayi, Richard Kozul-
Wright, Phillip Cobbina (research).

2006   Doubling Aid: Making the "Big Push" Work – UNCTAD/GDS/AFRICA/2006/1
Contributors: Kamran Kousari (team leader), Samuel Gayi, Richard Kozul-
Wright, Jane Harrigan (consultant), Victoria Chisala (research).

2007   Reclaiming Policy Space: Domestic Resource Mobilization and
Developmental States – UNCTAD/ALDC/AFRICA/2007
Contributors: Samuel Gayi (team leader), Janvier Nkurunziza, Martin Halle,
Shigehisa Kasahara.

2008   Export Performance Following Trade Liberalization: Some Patterns and
Policy Perspectives - UNCTAD/ALDC/AFRICA/2008
Contributors: Samuel Gayi (team leader), Janvier Nkurunziza, Martin Halle,
Shigehisa Kasahara.

2009   Strengthening Regional Economic Integration for Africa's Development - UNCTAD/ALDC/AFRICA/2009
        Contributors: Norbert Lebale (team leader), Janvier Nkurunziza, Martin Halle, Shigehisa Kasahara.

2010   South–South Cooperation: Africa and the New Forms of Development Partnership - UNCTAD/ALDC/AFRICA/2010
        Contributors: Norbert Lebale (team leader), Patrick Osakwe, Janvier Nkurunziza, Martin Halle, Michael Bratt and Adriano Timossi.

2011   Fostering Industrial Development in Africa in the New Global Environment - UNCTAD/ALDC/AFRICA/2011
        Contributors: Norbert Lebale (team leader), Patrick Osakwe, Bineswaree Bolaky, Milasoa Chérel-Robson and Philipp Neuerburg (UNIDO)

2012   Structural Transformation and Sustainable Development in Africa - UNCTAD/ALDC/AFRICA/2012
        Contributors: Charles Gore and Norbert Lebale (team leaders), Patrick Osakwe, Bineswaree Bolaky and Marko Sakai.

2013   Intra-African Trade: Unlocking Private Sector Dynamism - UNCTAD/ALDC/AFRICA/2013
        Contributors: Patrick Osakwe (team leader), Janvier Nkurunziza and Bineswaree Bolaky.

2014   Catalysing Investment for Transformative Growth in Africa - UNCTAD/ALDC/AFRICA/2014
        Contributors: Patrick Osakwe (team leader), Rashmi Banga and Bineswaree Bolaky.

2015   Unlocking the Potential of Africa's Services Trade for Growth and Development - UNCTAD/ALDC/AFRICA/2015
        Contributors: Junior Roy Davis (team leader), Laura Páez and Bineswaree Bolaky.

Copies of the series of reports on Economic Development in Africa may be obtained from the Division for Africa, Least Developed Countries and Special Programmes, UNCTAD, Palais des Nations, CH-1211 Geneva 10, Switzerland (e-mail: africadev@unctad.org). The reports are also accessible on the UNCTAD website at unctad.org/africa/series.